cook's library

vegetarian

cook's library

vegetarian

a collection of mouthwatering meals

p

This is a Parragon Book
This edition published in 2005

Parragon
Queen Street House
4 Queen Street
Bath BA1 1HE, UK

ISBN: 1-40544-627-7

Printed in Indonesia

NOTE

This book uses metric and imperial measurements. Follow the same
units of measurement throughout; do not mix metric and imperial.
All spoon measurements are level: teaspoons are assumed to be 5 ml,
and tablespoons are assumed to be 15 ml. Unless otherwise stated,
milk is assumed to be full fat, eggs and individual vegetables such as
potatoes are medium, and pepper is freshly ground black pepper.

The times given for each recipe are an approximate guide only because the
preparation times may differ according to the techniques used by different
people and the cooking times may vary as a result of the type of oven used.
The preparation times include chilling and marinating times, where appropriate.

Recipes using raw or very lightly cooked eggs should be
avoided by infants, the elderly, pregnant women, convalescents,
and anyone suffering from an illness.

Contents

Introduction

Vegetarian food need not be boring, as this inspirational cookbook will demonstrate! Packed full of delicious recipes that are nutritious and substantial, even the most discerning palate is sure to be satisfied.

Healthy Eating

Variety, of course, is the keynote to healthy eating, whatever the diet. As long as the day's meals contain a good mixture of different food types – carbohydrates, proteins and fats – a balanced diet and adequate supplies of essential vitamins and proteins are almost guaranteed. Typical dishes that are based on fresh vegetables, pulses, pasta or rice, for example, also have the advantage of being low in fats, particularly saturated fats, and high in complex carbohydrates and fibre, resulting in a diet that is in tune with modern nutritional thinking.

Vegetables are an important source of vitamins, especially vitamin C. Green vegetables and pulses contain many B-group vitamins. Both carrots and dark green vegetables contain high levels of carotene, which is used by the body to manufacture vitamin A. Carrots also contain useful quantities of vitamins B3, C and E. Vegetable oils contain vitamin E and most are also high in polyunsaturated fats. Vegetables are also a particularly good source of many essential minerals, especially calcium, iron, magnesium and potassium.

There is a long and honourable tradition of the specific, health-giving properties of different vegetables, which dates back at least as far as the Middle Ages. These qualities, once dismissed as old wives' tales, are now being recognized and valued again. Onions and garlic, for example, contain cycloallin, an anticoagulant that helps protect against heart disease. Garlic also contains a strong antibiotic, is thought to protect the body against some major diseases and also increases the absorption of many vitamins.

There is no question that a sensible vegetarian diet is at least as healthy as a sensible meat-eating diet and some nutritionists maintain that it is better. However, there are one or two particular points that are worth noting. Proteins are made up of 'building blocks' called amino acids and, while all those essential to the human body are easily obtained from most animal products, they are not always present in many vegetarian foods. A good mixed diet will prevent this from being a problem. For example, pulses are an excellent source of protein, but

they do lack one essential amino acid called methionine. Grains, on the other hand, contain this amino acid, although they lack two others, tryptophan and lysine. A dish that contains both rice and beans, a plate of hummus and pitta bread or a bowl of bean soup and a slice of wholemeal toast, for example, will ensure that all the necessary first-class proteins are available to the body.

Dairy products are also a valuable source of protein, but they are high in fat. It is very easy for busy people to fall into the habit of basing rather a lot of meals around cheese, for example, resulting in an unhealthily high intake of cholesterol. Eaten in moderation, however, cheese is a very useful and versatile ingredient in the vegetarian diet. If you do use dairy products a lot, it may be worth considering buying low-fat types, such as skimmed or semi-skimmed milk, fromage frais and soft cheeses.

It is important to be aware that the body cannot absorb iron from vegetable sources unless vitamin C is ingested at the same meal. Although many vegetables also contain vitamin C, this is easily destroyed through cooking. Some raw fruit, a glass of fruit juice or a side salad are simple and tasty solutions.

Vegans, who do not eat any dairy products, must be a little more scrupulous than straightforward vegetarians about ensuring that they obtain all the necessary nutrients. A lack of calcium, in particular, can be a problem, but this can be countered with a mineral supplement or by using calcium-enriched soya milk. A vegan diet may be just as healthy as a vegetarian or meat-eating one.

No foods can really be said to be bad for you, although some are best eaten in moderation. It is sensible to keep an eye on the quantities of butter, cream, high-fat cheeses, dried fruits, oils and unsalted nuts that you eat each day. Other popular vegetarian ingredients, such as grains, vegetables, pulses, fruit, bread, pasta and noodles can be eaten more freely. All diets should include raw vegetables and fruit and these should comprise as much as 40 per cent of a vegetarian diet.

Finally, a hidden advantage to changing to a vegetarian diet is that, usually, it initially entails thinking in a more detailed way about all the things you eat. This may extend across the whole spectrum of nutrition, including such things as your intake of salt, sugar and refined foods. As a result, many long-term vegetarians have developed eating patterns that are among the healthiest in the world.

Vegetables

Vegetables are, of course, at the heart of a vegetarian diet, offering an almost endless choice of flavours and textures. Preparing and cooking them with care ensures that they may be enjoyed at their best and that they retain their full nutritional value.

Buying

The fresher vegetables are, the better. Nevertheless, some, such as root vegetables, can be stored for relatively long periods in a cool, dark place and most will keep for two or three days in the salad drawer of the refrigerator. Supermarkets are very convenient and carry a wide range of good-quality vegetables, and finding a really high-quality supplier – possibly of organically-grown vegetables – will be repaid many times over in terms of flavour and nutritional value.

Whatever type you are buying, always look for unblemished and undamaged vegetables with no discoloration. Greens should have a good colour, with no wilting leaves, root vegetables should be firm and crisp, vegetable fruits, such as tomatoes and peppers, should not have soggy patches or wrinkled skin. No vegetables should ever look or smell stale.

Preparing

Use vegetables as soon after buying them as possible, but try not to prepare them much in advance of cooking. If they are left exposed to air or soaking in water, many vitamins and other valuable nutrients are leached out or destroyed.

The highest concentration of nutrients is in the layer directly under the skin, so if possible, avoid peeling them altogether. If they must be peeled, try to do it very thinly. A swivel vegetable peeler is a worthwhile investment. Also, consider cooking potatoes in their skins – first scrubbing off any soil or dirt – and peeling them afterwards. The skin comes off in a much thinner layer than when they are peeled raw.

How thickly or thinly vegetables are sliced, or how large or small they are chopped will depend, to some extent, on the method of cooking and the individual recipe instructions. However, remember that the smaller and finer the pieces, the greater the surface area from which nutrients can leach.

Green & Leafy Vegetables

Broad Beans

Top and tail and roughly slice very young beans that are less than 7.5 cm/3 inches long. Shell older beans and, if wished, skin after cooking.

Broccoli

Trim the stalk. Leave whole or break into florets – small 'flowers' with a little stalk attached – according to the recipe. Wash thoroughly.

Brussels Sprouts

Trim the end of the stalk and remove the outer leaves. Leave whole.

Cabbage

Remove the outer leaves, if necessary, cut in quarters and cut out the stem. Slice or shred according to the recipe.

Cauliflower

Cut off the thick stalk level with the base of the head and cut out the core. Remove larger, coarse leaves, but smaller ones can be left. Leave the head whole or break into florets.

Chinese Cabbage

Remove the outer leaves and slice the quantity required.

Green Beans

Top and tail young beans with kitchen scissors or a knife and leave whole. Snap off the ends of older beans and pull off any strings. Slice diagonally or shred before cooking.

Kale & Curly Kale

Break the leaves from the stalk, cut out thick stalks and cook whole or shredded.

Mangetouts

Top and tail, then leave whole.

Peas

Pop the fat end of the pod, split open and remove the peas. The pods of fresh, young peas boiled in water make an excellent light stock for soups.

Runner Beans

Top, tail and string, then slice lengthways. A bean-slicer is good for this task.

Spinach

Rinse thoroughly, taking care not to bruise the delicate leaves. Use two changes of cold water and drain, then pull or cut off any tough stalks.

Shoots and Stems

Asparagus

Trim the woody end of the stalk. White asparagus stems usually require peeling.

Celery

Trim the base and separate the stalks. Wash thoroughly and slice thickly or thinly. If using raw in a salad, pull off any coarse strings. The leaves, when chopped, add flavour to soups and casseroles and also make an attractive garnish.

Fennel

Remove the outer layer of skin, except from very young bulbs. Slice downwards or horizontally according to the recipe. Use the fronds for a garnish.

Globe Artichokes

Twist off the stem and cut the base flat, removing any small, spiky leaves. Cut off the top 1 cm and trim the points of the remaining leaves.

Root Vegetables

Carrots

Trim the ends and scrub young carrots, as they do not need peeling. They may be left whole, sliced or diced. Thinly peel older carrots and, if necessary, cut out the woody core.

Celeriac

Peel off the thick skin immediately before cooking, as the flesh quickly discolours. Slice or chop according to the recipe. If necessary, put the pieces into a bowl of water acidulated with a little lemon juice.

Jerusalem Artichokes

Scrub in cold water and cook in their skins before peeling. Otherwise peel immediately before use, placing them in water acidulated with a little lemon juice to prevent discoloration.

Leeks

Trim the root and the dark leaves. Cut in half lengthways or prepare according to the recipe and wash well in plenty of cold water. Drain thoroughly.

Onions & Shallots

Peel off the papery skin, trim and slice or chop according to the recipe.

Parsnips

Trim and thinly peel. Small parsnips may be left whole; older parsnips may be halved, sliced or diced according to the recipe.

Potatoes

Wash new potatoes in cold running water and cook in their skins, as they do not need peeling. Scrub old potatoes and either cook in their skins, depending on the method, and peel afterwards, or thinly peel before cooking.

Spring Onions

Trim the root and cut off any wilted green leaves. Slice or chop according to the recipe.

Swedes

Trim and peel off the thick skin. Chop or dice according to the recipe instructions.

Sweet Potatoes

Scrub and cook in their skins and peel afterwards or thinly peel and put in water acidulated with a little lemon juice.

Salad Vegetables

Chicory

Using a sharp, pointed knife, remove the core from the base. Discard any wilted leaves, then wash and dry thoroughly.

Cucumbers

Wash and peel, if liked. Always peel glossy, waxed cucumbers. Slice thinly or dice for salads. If cooking cucumber, first cut into wedges and remove the seeds. Peeling strips, while leaving a strip of skin between, creates a decorative edge when sliced.

Escarole

Separate the leaves and discard any that are discoloured. Wash thoroughly and pat dry.

Lettuce

Separate the leaves and wash in several changes of water. Adding vinegar to the first rinse will kill any insects in lettuces grown outdoors. Spin in a salad dryer or wrap in a clean tea towel and shake dry. Tear loose-leafed lettuces into smaller pieces and slice or shred firm lettuce. Buying mixed bags of lettuce gives a good selection of leaves.

Vegetable Fruits

Aubergines

Newer varieties no longer require salting to remove the bitter taste; they are not so bitter as older varieties. However, salting still helps to draw out some of the moisture. Wash the aubergine, cut into slices or segments, according to the recipe, place in a colander and sprinkle generously with salt. Leave for 30 minutes, rinse well and pat dry with kitchen paper.

Avocados

Halve and remove the stone, then sprinkle the flesh with lemon juice to prevent discoloration. Leave in halves for serving with a vinaigrette. For other dishes, slice and then peel, or dice in the shells and then scoop out the diced flesh. (Peeled avocados are slippery and difficult to handle.)

Peppers

For stuffing, cut a slice from the top, cut out the inner core and shake out any remaining seeds. For other dishes, halve and remove the core and seeds, then quarter, slice or dice. To peel peppers, halve or quarter and grill, skin side up, until charred and beginning to blister. Transfer the pieces of pepper to a plastic bag, seal and set aside for 5–10 minutes. The skin will peel easily.

Tomatoes

Wash well. To peel, cut a cross in the skin at the base, briefly blanch in boiling water and rinse in cold water. The skin should then peel off easily. Cut salad tomatoes and those for pizza toppings horizontally.

Mooli

Trim and wash, then slice, dice or grate, according to the recipe.

Radicchio

Separate the leaves and discard any that are discoloured. Wash thoroughly and pat dry.

Radishes

Wash and leave whole or slice.

Rocket

Discard any discoloured leaves and wash the remainder.

Watercress

Discard any wilted leaves and remove any thick stalks. Wash thoroughly.

Squashes

Courgettes

Leave baby courgettes whole – with their flowers. Top and tail, then slice, dice or stuff, according to the recipe. Used separately, the flowers can be fried in a light batter until crisp and golden.

Pumpkins

Peel, deseed and chop. It may be easier to lightly cook, before peeling, depending on the recipe.

Summer Squashes

Wash, then peel if the skin is tough or if the vegetable is to be braised or sautéed.

How to Use This Book

Each recipe contains a wealth of useful information, including a breakdown
of nutritional quantities, preparation and cooking times, and level of difficulty.
All of this information is explained in detail below.

A full-colour photograph
of the finished dish.

The ingredients for
each recipe are listed
in the order that they
are used.

The nutritional
information provided
for each recipe is per
serving or per portion.
Optional ingredients,
variations or serving
suggestions have not
been included in the
calculations.

The method is clearly
explained with step-by-
step instructions that
are easy to follow.

Cook's tips provide useful
information regarding
ingredients or cooking
techniques.

A wonderful mixture of red lentils, tofu and vegetables is cooked beneath a crunchy potato topping for a really hearty meal.

Potato-Topped Lentil Bake

SERVES 4

Topping
675 g/1 lb 8 oz floury potatoes, diced
25 g/1 oz butter
1 tbsp milk
50 g/1¾ oz chopped pecan nuts
2 tbsp chopped fresh thyme
fresh thyme sprigs, to garnish

Filling
225 g/8 oz red lentils, washed
55 g/2 oz butter
1 leek, sliced
2 garlic cloves, crushed
1 celery stick, chopped
125 g/4½ oz broccoli florets
175 g/6 oz smoked tofu, cubed
2 tsp tomato puree
salt and pepper

1 To make the topping, cook the diced potatoes in a saucepan of boiling water for 10–15 minutes, or until cooked through. Drain well, add the butter and milk and mash thoroughly. Stir in the choped pecan nuts and the chopped thyme and set aside.

2 Cook the lentils in boiling water for 20–30 minutes, or until tender. Drain and set aside.

3 Melt the butter in a frying pan. Add the leek, garlic, celery and broccoli. Fry over a medium heat, stirring frequently for 5 minutes, until softened.

4 Add the tofu cubes. Stir in the lentils, together with the tomato puree. Season with salt and pepper to taste, then turn the mixture into the base of a shallow ovenproof dish.

5 Spoon the mashed potato on top of the lentil mixture, spreading to cover it completely.

6 Cook the lentil bake in a preheated oven, 200°C/400°F/Gas Mark 6, for about 30–35 minutes, or until the topping is golden brown. Remove the bake from the oven, garnish with fresh thyme sprigs and serve hot.

NUTRITION
Calories 627, Sugars 7 g, Protein 26 g,
Carbohydrate 66 g, Fat 30 g, Saturates 13 g

⊙⊙⊙ moderate
🕐 10 mins
🕐 1 hr 30 mins

COOK'S TIP
You can use almost any combination of your favourite vegetables in this dish.

⭐ The number of stars represents the
difficulty of each recipe, ranging from
very easy (1 star) to challenging (4 stars).

🕐 This amount of time represents the
preparation of ingredients, including
cooling, chilling and soaking times.

🕐 This represents the cooking time.

Basic Recipes

These recipes form the basis of several of the dishes contained in this book. Many of these basic recipes can be made in advance and stored in the refrigerator until required.

Fresh Vegetable Stock

225 g/8 oz shallots
1 large carrot, diced
1 celery stick, chopped
½ fennel bulb
1 garlic clove
1 bay leaf
a few fresh parsley and tarragon sprigs
2 litres/3½ pints water
pepper

1 Put all of the ingredients in a large saucepan and bring to the boil. Skim off the surface scum with a flat spoon and reduce to a gentle simmer. Partially cover and cook for 45 minutes. Leave to cool.

2 Line a sieve with clean muslin and put over a large jug or bowl. Pour the stock through the sieve. Discard the herbs and vegetables. Cover and store in small quantities in the refrigerator for up to 3 days.

Béchamel Sauce

600 ml/1 pint milk
4 whole cloves
1 bay leaf
pinch of freshly grated nutmeg
25 g/1 oz butter or margarine
25 g/1 oz plain flour
salt and pepper

1 Put the milk in a saucepan and add the cloves, bay leaf and nutmeg. Gradually bring to the boil. Remove from the heat and leave for 15 minutes.

2 Melt the butter or margarine in another saucepan and stir in the flour to make a roux. Cook, stirring, for 1 minute. Remove the pan from the heat.

3 Strain the milk and gradually blend into the roux. Return the pan to the heat and bring to the boil, stirring, until the sauce thickens. Season with salt and pepper to taste and add any flavourings.

Tahini Cream

3 tbsp tahini
6 tbsp water
2 tsp lemon juice
1 garlic clove, crushed
salt and pepper

1 Blend together the tahini and water.

2 Stir in the lemon juice and garlic. Season with salt and pepper to taste. The tahini cream is now ready to serve.

Tomato Sauce

2 tbsp olive oil
1 small onion, chopped
1 garlic clove, crushed
400 g/14 oz canned tomatoes
1 tbsp chopped fresh basil
1 bay leaf
2 tbsp tomato purée
1 tsp sugar
salt and pepper

1 Heat the oil in a pan. Fry the onion until translucent. Add the garlic and cook for another minute.

2 Stir in the tomatoes, basil, bay leaf, tomato purée and sugar and season to taste.

3 Bring to the boil, reduce the heat and simmer for 15–20 minutes or until reduced by half. Discard the bay leaf and adjust the seasoning.

Green Herb Dressing

15 g/½ oz fresh parsley

15 g/½ oz fresh mint

15 g/½ oz fresh chives

1 garlic clove, crushed

150 ml/5 floz natural yogurt

salt and pepper

1 Remove the stalks from the parsley and mint and put the leaves in a blender or food processor.

2 Add the chives, garlic and yogurt and salt and pepper to taste. Blend until smooth, then store in the refrigerator until needed.

Sesame Dressing

2 tbsp tahini (sesame seed paste)

2 tbsp cider vinegar

2 tbsp medium sherry

2 tbsp sesame oil

1 tbsp soy sauce

1 garlic clove, crushed

1 Put the tahini (sesame seed paste) in a bowl and gradually mix in the vinegar and sherry until smooth. Add the sesame oil, soy sauce and garlic and mix together thoroughly.

Cucumber Dressing

200 g/7 oz natural yogurt

5-cm/2-inch piece of cucumber, peeled

1 tbsp chopped fresh mint leaves

½ tsp grated lemon rind

pinch of caster sugar

salt and pepper

1 Put the yogurt, cucumber, mint, lemon rind, sugar and salt and pepper to taste in a blender or food processor and work until smooth. Alternatively, finely chop the cucumber and combine with the other ingredients. Serve chilled.

Apple and Cider Vinegar Dressing

2 tbsp sunflower oil

2 tbsp concentrated apple juice

2 tbsp cider vinegar

1 tbsp Meaux mustard

1 garlic clove, crushed

salt and pepper

1 Put the oil, apple juice, cider vinegar, mustard, garlic and salt and pepper to taste in a screw-top jar and shake vigorously until well-mixed.

Warm Walnut Dressing

6 tbsp walnut oil

3 tbsp white wine vinegar

1 tbsp clear honey

1 tsp wholegrain mustard

1 garlic clove, sliced

salt and pepper

1 Put the oil, vinegar, honey, mustard and salt and pepper to taste in a saucepan and whisk together.

2 Add the garlic and heat very gently for 3 minutes. Remove the garlic slices with a slotted spoon and discard. Pour the dressing over the salad and serve immediately.

Tomato Dressing

125 ml/4 fl oz tomato juice

1 garlic clove, crushed

2 tbsp lemon juice

1 tbsp soy sauce

1 tsp clear honey

2 tbsp chopped fresh chives

salt and pepper

1 Put the tomato juice, garlic, lemon juice, soy sauce, honey, chives and salt and pepper to taste in a screw-top jar and shake vigorously until well-mixed.

Soups

Soup is easy to make, but always produces delicious results. There is an enormous variety of soups which you can make with vegetables. They can be rich and creamy, thick and chunky, light and delicate, and hot or chilled. The vegetables are often puréed to give a smooth consistency and thicken the soup, but you can also purée just some of the mixture to give the soup more texture and interest. A wide range of ingredients can be used in addition to vegetables – pulses, grains, noodles, cheese and yogurt all work well. You can also experiment with different substitutions if you don't have certain ingredients to hand. Whatever your preference, you're sure to enjoy the variety of tasty soups contained in this chapter. Serve with fresh bread for a delicious meal.

A thick vegetable soup which is a delicious meal in itself. Serve the soup with thin shavings of Parmesan and warm ciabatta bread.

Winter Soup

SERVES 4

2 tbsp olive oil
2 leeks, sliced thinly
2 courgettes, chopped
2 garlic cloves, crushed
800 g/1 lb 12 oz canned chopped tomatoes
1 tbsp tomato purée
1 bay leaf
900 ml/1½ pints Fresh Vegetable Stock
(see page 16)
400 g/14 oz canned chickpeas, drained
225 g/8 oz spinach
25 g/1 oz Parmesan cheese, shaved thinly
salt and pepper
crusty bread, to serve

1 Heat the oil in a heavy-based saucepan. Add the sliced leeks and courgettes and cook over a medium heat, stirring constantly, for 5 minutes.

2 Add the garlic, chopped tomatoes, tomato purée, bay leaf, vegetable stock and chickpeas. Bring to the boil, lower the heat and simmer, stirring occasionally, for 5 minutes.

3 Shred the spinach finely and add it to the soup. Cook the soup for a further 2 minutes over a medium-high heat, until the spinach is just wilted. Season to taste with salt and pepper.

4 Remove the bay leaf. Pour the soup into a warmed tureen or individual bowls and sprinkle over the Parmesan. Serve with crusty bread.

NUTRITION
Calories 285; Sugars 11 g; Protein 16 g;
Carbohydrate 29 g; Fat 12 g; Saturates 3 g

  very easy

10 mins

20 mins

Homemade tomato soup is easy to make and often tastes better than bought varieties. Try this version with its sunny Mediterranean influences.

Plum Tomato Soup

1 Heat the oil in a large saucepan. Add the onions, celery and carrot and fry over a low heat, stirring frequently, until softened, but not coloured.

2 Add the tomatoes, stock, chopped herbs, wine and sugar. Bring to the boil, cover and simmer for 20 minutes.

3 Place the toasted hazelnuts in a blender or food processor, together with the olives and basil leaves, and process until thoroughly combined, but not too smooth. Alternatively, finely chop the nuts, olives and basil leaves and pound them together in a mortar with a pestle, then turn into a small bowl. Add the olive oil and process or beat thoroughly for a few seconds to combine. Turn the mixture into a serving bowl.

4 Warm the ciabatta bread in a preheated oven, 190°C/375°F/ Gas Mark 5, for 3–4 minutes.

5 Process the soup in a blender or a food processor, or press through a sieve, until smooth, Check the seasoning. Ladle into warmed soup bowls and garnish with basil sprigs. Slice the warm bread and spread with the olive and hazelnut paste. Serve with the soup.

SERVES 4

2 tbsp olive oil
2 red onions, chopped
2 celery sticks, chopped
1 carrot, chopped
500 g/1 lb 2 oz plum tomatoes, halved
750 ml/1¼ pints Fresh Vegetable Stock
   (see page 16)
1 tbsp chopped fresh oregano
1 tbsp chopped fresh basil
150 ml/5 fl oz dry white wine
2 tsp caster sugar
125 g/4½ oz hazelnuts, toasted
125 g/4½ oz black or green olives
handful of fresh basil leaves
1 tbsp olive oil
1 loaf ciabatta bread
salt and pepper
fresh basil sprigs, to garnish

NUTRITION
Calories 402; Sugars 14 g; Protein 7 g;
Carbohydrate 16 g; Fat 32 g; Saturates 3 g

 very easy
 20 mins
 30–35 mins

This Spanish soup is full of chopped and grated vegetables with a puréed tomato base. It requires chilling, so prepare well in advance.

Gazpacho

SERVES 4

½ small cucumber
½ small green pepper, halved, deseeded and chopped finely
500 g/1 lb 2 oz ripe tomatoes, peeled or 400 g/14 oz canned chopped tomatoes
½ onion, chopped coarsely
2–3 garlic cloves, crushed
3 tbsp olive oil
2 tbsp white wine vinegar
1–2 tbsp lemon or lime juice
2 tbsp tomato purée
450 ml/16 fl oz tomato juice
salt and pepper

to serve
chopped green pepper
sliced thinly onion rings
garlic croûtons

1 Coarsely grate the cucumber into a large bowl and add the green pepper.

2 Put the tomatoes, onion and garlic in a food processor or blender, add the oil, vinegar, lemon juice and tomato purée, and process until a smooth purée is formed. Alternatively, finely chop the tomatoes and finely grate the onion, then mix together and add the crushed garlic, oil, vinegar, lemon juice and tomato purée.

3 Add the tomato mixture to the bowl and mix well, then add the tomato juice and mix again.

4 Season to taste, cover the bowl with clear film and chill for at least 6 hours, preferably longer, so that the flavours have time to meld together.

5 Prepare the side dishes of chopped green pepper, sliced thinly onion rings and garlic croûtons, and arrange them in individual serving bowls.

6 Ladle the soup into chilled bowls, preferably from a soup tureen set on the table with the side dishes of pepper, onion rings and croûtons placed around it. Hand the dishes around to allow the guests to help themselves.

NUTRITION
Calories *140*; Sugars *12 g*; Protein *3 g*;
Carbohydrate *13 g*; Fat *9 g*; Saturates *1 g*

 very easy
 6 hrs 30 mins
0 mins

This is an American classic that has now become popular worldwide. When pumpkin is out of season, use butternut squash in its place.

Pumpkin Soup

1 Peel the pumpkin, remove the seeds and then cut the flesh into 2.5-cm/1-inch cubes.

2 Melt the butter or margarine in a large, heavy-based saucepan. Add the onion and garlic and fry over a low heat until soft, but not coloured.

3 Add the pumpkin and toss with the onion for 2–3 minutes.

4 Add the stock and bring to the boil over a medium heat. Season to taste with salt and pepper and add the ground ginger and lemon juice, the strips of orange rind, if using, and the bay leaves or bouquet garni.

5 Cover the pan and gently simmer the soup over a low heat for about 20 minutes, stirring occasionally, until the pumpkin is tender.

6 Discard the orange rind, if using, and the bay leaves or bouquet garni. Cool the soup slightly, then press through a sieve with the back of a spoon, or process in a food processor until smooth. Pour into a clean saucepan.

7 Add the milk and reheat gently. Adjust the seasoning. Garnish with a swirl of cream, and snipped chives, and serve.

SERVES 6

about 1 kg/2 lb 4 oz pumpkin
40 g/1½ oz butter or margarine
1 onion, thinly sliced
1 garlic clove, crushed
900 ml/1½ pints Fresh Vegetable Stock (see page 16)
½ tsp ground ginger
1 tbsp lemon juice
3–4 thinly pared strips of orange rind (optional)
1–2 bay leaves or 1 bouquet garni
300 ml/10 fl oz milk
salt and pepper

to garnish
4–6 tablespoons single or double cream, natural yogurt or fromage frais
snipped fresh chives

NUTRITION
Calories *112*; Sugars *7 g*; Protein *4 g*; Carbohydrate *8 g*; Fat *7 g*; Saturates *2 g*

 very easy

 10 mins

 30 mins

This soup has a real
Mediterranean flavour,
using sweet red peppers,
tomato, chilli and basil.
It is great served with
olive bread.

Pepper *and* Chilli Soup

S E R V E S   4

225 g/8 oz red peppers, halved, deseeded
   and sliced
1 onion, sliced
2 garlic cloves, crushed
1 fresh green chilli, chopped
300 ml/10 fl oz passata
600 ml/1 pint Fresh Vegetable Stock
   (see page 16)
2 tbsp chopped basil
fresh basil sprigs, to garnish

1 Put the red peppers in a large saucepan with the onion, garlic and chilli. Add
the passata and the vegetable stock and bring to the boil, stirring well.

2 Reduce the heat to a simmer and continue to cook the vegetables for
20 minutes, or until the peppers have softened. Drain, reserving the liquid
and vegetables separately.

3 Using the back of a spoon, press the vegetables through a sieve.
Alternatively, process in a food processor until smooth.

4 Return the vegetable purée to a clean saucepan with the reserved cooking
liquid. Add the basil and heat through until hot. Garnish the soup with fresh
basil sprigs and serve immediately.

N U T R I T I O N
Calories 55; Sugars 10 g; Protein 2 g;
Carbohydrate 11 g; Fat 0.5 g; Saturates 0.1 g

⭐ very easy

🕐 10 mins

🕐 25 mins

 C O O K ' S   T I P

This soup is also delicious served cold with 150 ml/5 fl oz of natural yogurt
swirled into it.

Full of flavour, this rich and creamy soup is very simple to make and utterly delicious to eat.

Stilton *and* Walnut Soup

1 Melt the butter in a large, heavy-based saucepan and sauté the shallots, celery and garlic together, stirring occasionally, for 2–3 minutes, until they are softened.

2 Lower the heat, add the flour and continue to cook, stirring constantly, for a further 30 seconds.

3 Gradually stir in the vegetable stock and milk and bring to the boil.

4 Reduce the heat to a gentle simmer and add the crumbled blue Stilton cheese and walnut halves. Cover and simmer for 20 minutes.

5 Stir in the yogurt and heat through for a further 2 minutes, but be careful not to let the soup boil.

6 Season the soup to taste with salt and pepper, then transfer to a warm soup tureen or individual serving bowls, garnish with chopped celery leaves and extra crumbled blue Stilton cheese and serve at once.

SERVES 4

55 g/2 oz butter
2 shallots, chopped
3 celery sticks, chopped
1 garlic clove, crushed
2 tbsp plain flour
600 ml/1 pint Fresh Vegetable Stock (see page 16)
300 ml/10 fl oz milk
150 g/5½ oz blue Stilton cheese, crumbled, plus extra to garnish
2 tbsp walnut halves, chopped roughly
150 ml/5 fl oz natural yogurt
salt and pepper
chopped celery leaves, to garnish

NUTRITION
Calories 392; Sugars 8 g; Protein 15 g; Carbohydrate 15 g; Fat 30 g; Saturates 16 g

 moderate
 15 mins
15 mins
20 mins

🍵 COOK'S TIP

As well as adding protein, vitamins and useful fats to the diet, nuts add important flavour and texture to vegetarian meals.

A delicious creamy soup with grated carrot and parsley for texture and colour. Serve with crusty cheese scones for a hearty lunch.

Thick Onion Soup

SERVES 4

75 g/2³/₄ oz butter
500 g/1 lb 2 oz onions, chopped finely
1 garlic clove, crushed
40 g/1¹/₂ oz plain flour
600 ml/1 pint Fresh Vegetable Stock
 (see page 16)
600 ml/1 pint milk
2–3 tsp lemon or lime juice
good pinch of ground allspice
1 bay leaf
1 carrot, coarsely grated
4–6 tbsp double cream
salt and pepper
2 tbsp chopped fresh parsley, to garnish

cheese scones
225 g/8 oz wholemeal flour
2 tsp baking powder
55 g/2 oz butter
4 tbsp grated Parmesan cheese
1 egg, beaten
about 75 ml/2¹/₂ fl oz milk

NUTRITION

Calories 277; Sugars 12 g; Protein 6 g;
Carbohydrate 19 g; Fat 20 g; Saturates 8 g

easy
20 mins
1 hr 10 mins

1 Melt the butter in a saucepan and fry the onions and garlic over a low heat, stirring frequently, for 10–15 minutes, until soft, but not coloured. Stir in the flour and cook, for 1 minute, then gradually stir in the stock and bring to the boil, stirring frequently. Add the milk, then bring back to the boil.

2 Season to taste with salt and pepper and add 2 teaspoons of the lemon juice, the allspice and bay leaf. Cover and simmer for about 25 minutes until the vegetables are tender. Discard the bay leaf.

3 Meanwhile, make the scones. Combine the flour, baking powder and seasoning and rub in the butter, until the mixture resembles fine breadcrumbs. Stir in 3 tablespoons of the cheese, the egg and enough milk to mix to a soft dough.

4 Shape into a bar about 2-cm/¹/₄-inch thick. Place on a floured baking tray and mark into slices. Sprinkle with the remaining cheese and bake in a preheated oven, 220°C/425°F/Gas Mark 7, for about 20 minutes, until risen and golden.

5 Stir the carrot into the soup and simmer for 2–3 minutes. Add more lemon juice, if necessary. Stir in the cream and reheat. Garnish with chopped parsley and serve with the warm scones.

Parsnips make a delicious soup as they have a slightly sweet flavour. In this recipe, spices are added to complement this sweetness.

Curried Parsnip Soup

1 Heat the oil and butter in a large saucepan until the butter has melted. Add the onion, parsnips and garlic and sauté, stirring frequently, for about 5–7 minutes, until the vegetables have softened, but not coloured.

2 Add the garam masala and chilli powder and cook, stirring constantly, for 30 seconds. Sprinkle in the flour, mixing well and cook, stirring constantly, for a further 30 seconds.

3 Stir in the stock, lemon rind and juice and bring to the boil. Reduce the heat and simmer for 20 minutes.

4 Remove some of the vegetable pieces with a slotted spoon and reserve until required. Transfer the remaining soup and vegetables to a food processor or blender and process for about 1 minute, or until a smooth purée is formed. Alternatively, press the vegetables through a sieve with the back of a wooden spoon.

5 Return the soup to a clean saucepan and stir in the reserved vegetables. Heat the soup through for 2 minutes until piping hot.

6 Season to taste with salt and pepper, then transfer to soup bowls, garnish with grated lemon rind and serve.

SERVES **4**

1 tbsp vegetable oil
15 g/½ oz butter
1 red onion, chopped
3 parsnips, chopped
2 garlic cloves, crushed
2 tsp garam masala
½ tsp chilli powder
1 tbsp plain flour
850 ml/1½ pints Fresh Vegetable Stock (see page 16)
grated rind and juice of 1 lemon
salt and pepper
lemon rind, to garnish

NUTRITION
Calories 152; Sugars 7 g; Protein 3 g; Carbohydrate 18 g; Fat 8 g; Saturates 3 g

⭐   very easy
     10 mins
     35 mins

Spinach is the basis for this delicious soup, which has creamy mascarpone cheese stirred through it to give it a wonderful texture.

Spinach *and* Mascarpone Soup

S E R V E S 4

55 g/2 oz butter
1 bunch spring onions, trimmed
   and chopped
2 celery sticks, chopped
350 g/12 oz spinach or sorrel, or
   3 bunches watercress
850 ml/1½ pints Fresh Vegetable Stock
   (see page 16)
225 g/8 oz mascarpone cheese
1 tbsp olive oil
2 slices thick-cut bread, cut into cubes
½ tsp caraway seeds
salt and pepper
sesame bread sticks, to serve

1 Melt half the butter in a very large saucepan. Add the spring onions and celery, and cook over a medium heat, stirring frequently, for about 5 minutes, until softened.

2 Pack the spinach, into the saucepan. Add the stock and bring to the boil, then reduce the heat, cover and simmer for 15–20 minutes.

3 Transfer the soup to a blender or food processor and process until smooth. Alternatively, rub it through a sieve. Return to the saucepan.

4 Add the mascarpone to the soup and heat gently, stirring constantly, until smooth and blended. Season to taste with salt and pepper.

5 Heat the remaining butter with the oil in a frying pan. Add the bread cubes and fry, turning frequently, until golden brown, adding the caraway seeds towards the end of cooking, so that they do not burn.

6 Ladle the soup into warmed bowls. Sprinkle with the croûtons and serve with the sesame bread sticks.

N U T R I T I O N
Calories *402*; Sugars *2 g*; Protein *11 g*;
Carbohydrate *10 g*; Fat *36 g*; Saturates *21 g*

  very easy

15 mins

30 mins

🍲 **C O O K ' S T I P**

Any leafy vegetable can be used to vary the flavour of this soup. For anyone who grows their own vegetables, it is the perfect recipe for experimenting with a glut. Try young beetroot leaves or surplus lettuces for a change.

A quick chunky soup, ideal for a snack or a quick lunch. Save some of the soup and purée it to make one portion of creamed soup for the next day.

Leek, Potato *and* Carrot Soup

1 Trim off and discard some of the coarse green part of the leek, then slice thinly and rinse thoroughly in cold water. Drain well.

2 Heat the sunflower oil in a heavy-based saucepan. Add the leek and garlic, and fry over a low heat for about 2–3 minutes, until soft, but barely coloured. Add the vegetable stock, bay leaf and cumin and season to taste with salt and pepper. Bring the mixture to the boil, stirring constantly.

3 Add the diced potato to the saucepan, cover and simmer over a low heat for 10–15 minutes. Keep a careful eye on the soup during the cooking time to make sure the potato cooks until it is just tender, but not broken up.

4 Add the grated carrot to the pan and simmer the soup for a further 2–3 minutes. Adjust the seasoning if necessary, discard the bay leaf and serve the soup in warmed bowls, sprinkled liberally with the chopped parsley.

5 To make a puréed soup, first process the leftovers (about half the original soup) in a blender or food processor, or press through a sieve with the back of a wooden spoon until smooth, and then return to a clean saucepan with the milk. Bring to the boil and simmer for 2–3 minutes.

6 Adjust the seasoning and stir in the cream or crème fraîche before serving the soup in warmed bowls, sprinkled with chopped parsley.

SERVES 2

1 leek, about 175 g/6 oz in total
1 tbsp sunflower oil
1 garlic clove, crushed
700 ml/1¼ pints Fresh Vegetable Stock (see page 16)
1 bay leaf
¼ tsp ground cumin
175 g/6 oz potatoes, diced
125 g/4½ oz coarsely grated carrot
salt and pepper
chopped fresh parsley, to garnish

puréed soup
5–6 tbsp milk
1–2 tbsp double cream, crème fraîche or soured cream

NUTRITION
Calories 156; Sugars 7 g; Protein 4 g; Carbohydrate 22 g; Fat 6 g; Saturates 0.7g g

  very easy
  10 mins
       25 mins

This creamy soup has a delightful pale green colouring and rich flavour from the blend of tender broccoli and blue cheese.

Broccoli *and* Potato Soup

SERVES 4

2 tbsp olive oil
450 g/1 lb potatoes, diced
1 onion, diced
225 g/8 oz broccoli florets
125 g/4½ oz blue cheese, crumbled
1 litre/1¾ pints Fresh Vegetable Stock
    (see page 16)
150 ml/5 fl oz double cream
pinch of paprika
salt and pepper

1 Heat the oil in a large saucepan. Add the potatoes and onion. Sauté, stirring constantly, for 5 minutes.

2 Reserve a few broccoli florets for the garnish and add the remaining broccoli to the pan. Add the cheese and the vegetable stock.

3 Bring to the boil, then reduce the heat, cover the pan and simmer for 25 minutes, until the potatoes are tender.

4 Transfer the soup to a food processor or blender in batches and process until the mixture is smooth. Alternatively, press the vegetables through a sieve with the back of a wooden spoon.

5 Return the purée to a clean saucepan and stir in the double cream and a pinch of paprika. Season to taste with salt and pepper.

6 Blanch the reserved broccoli florets in a little boiling water for about 2 minutes, then lift them out of the pan with a slotted spoon.

7 Pour the soup into warmed individual bowls and garnish with the broccoli florets and a sprinkling of paprika. Serve the soup immediately.

NUTRITION
Calories 452; Sugars 4 g; Protein 14 g;
Carbohydrate 20 g; Fat 35 g; Saturates 19 g

moderate

5–10 mins

35 mins

🍲 **COOK'S TIP**

This soup freezes very successfully. Follow the method described here up to step 4, and freeze the soup after it has been puréed. Add the cream and paprika just before serving. Garnish and serve.

A slightly hot and spicy Indian flavour is given to this soup through the use of garam masala, chilli, cumin and coriander.

Indian Potato *and* Pea Soup

1 Heat the vegetable oil in a large saucepan. Add the potatoes, onion and garlic and sauté over a low heat, stirring constantly, for about 5 minutes.

2 Add the garam masala, coriander and cumin and cook, stirring constantly, for 1 minute.

3 Stir in the vegetable stock and red chilli and bring the mixture to the boil. Reduce the heat, cover the pan and simmer for 20 minutes, until the potatoes begin to break down.

4 Add the peas and cook for a further 5 minutes. Stir in the yogurt and season to taste with salt and pepper.

5 Pour into warmed soup bowls, garnish with chopped fresh coriander and serve hot with warm bread.

SERVES 4

2 tbsp vegetable oil
225 g/8 oz floury potatoes, diced
1 large onion, chopped
2 garlic cloves, crushed
1 tsp garam masala
1 tsp ground coriander
1 tsp ground cumin
850 ml/1½ pints Fresh Vegetable Stock
(see page 16)
1 red chilli, chopped
100 g/3½ oz frozen peas
4 tbsp natural yogurt
salt and pepper
chopped fresh coriander, to garnish
warm bread, to serve

NUTRITION
Calories 153; Sugars 6 g; Protein 6 g; Carbohydrate 18 g; Fat 6 g; Saturates 1 g

moderate
15 mins
20 mins

COOK'S TIP

For slightly less heat, deseed the chilli before adding it to the soup. Always wash your hands after handling chillies because they contain volatile oils that can irritate the skin and make your eyes burn if you touch your face.

Fresh asparagus is now available for most of the year, so this soup can be made at any time. It can also be made using canned asparagus.

Asparagus Soup

SERVES 6

1 bunch asparagus, about 350 g/12 oz, or 2 packs mini asparagus, about 150 g/5½ oz each
700 ml/1¼ pints Fresh Vegetable Stock (see page 16)
55 g/2 oz butter or margarine
1 onion, chopped
3 tbsp plain flour
¼ tsp ground coriander
1 tbsp lemon juice
450 ml/16 fl oz milk
4–6 tbsp double or single cream
salt and pepper

1 Wash and trim the asparagus, discarding the lower, woody part of the stem. Cut the remainder into short lengths, keeping aside a few tips to use as a garnish. Mini asparagus does not need to be trimmed.

2 Cook the tips in the minimum of boiling salted water for 5–10 minutes. Drain and set aside.

3 Put the asparagus in a saucepan with the stock, bring to the boil, cover and simmer for about 20 minutes, until soft. Drain and reserve the stock.

4 Melt the butter or margarine in a saucepan. Add the onion and fry over a low heat until soft, but only barely coloured. Stir in the flour and cook for 1 minute, then gradually whisk in the reserved stock and bring to the boil.

5 Simmer for 2–3 minutes, until thickened, then stir in the cooked asparagus, seasoning, coriander and lemon juice. Simmer for 10 minutes, then cool a little and either press through a sieve with the back of a spoon or process in a blender or food processor until smooth.

6 Pour into a clean pan, add the milk and reserved asparagus tips and bring to the boil. Simmer for 2 minutes. Stir in the cream, reheat gently and serve.

NUTRITION
Calories 196; Sugars 7 g; Protein 7 g; Carbohydrate 15 g; Fat 12 g; Saturates 4 g

 very easy
 5–10 mins
 55 mins

🍲 COOK'S TIP

If using canned asparagus, drain off the liquid and use as part of the measured stock. Remove a few small asparagus tips for garnish and chop the remainder. Continue from step 3.

Avocado has a rich flavour and colour which makes a creamy flavoured soup. It is best served chilled, but may be eaten warm.

Avocado *and* Vegetable Soup

1 Peel the avocado and mash the flesh with a fork, stir in the lemon juice and reserve until required.

2 Heat the vegetable oil in a large saucepan. Add the sweetcorn, tomatoes, garlic, leek and chilli and sauté over a low heat for 2–3 minutes, or until the vegetables have softened.

3 Put half the vegetable mixture in a food processor or blender, together with the mashed avocado, and process until smooth. Transfer the mixture to a clean saucepan.

4 Add the vegetable stock, milk and reserved vegetables and cook over a low heat for 3–4 minutes, until hot. Transfer to warmed individual serving bowls, garnish with shredded leek and serve immediately.

SERVES 4

1 large, ripe avocado
2 tbsp lemon juice
1 tbsp vegetable oil
50 g/1¼ oz canned sweetcorn, drained
2 tomatoes, peeled and deseeded
1 garlic clove, crushed
1 leek, chopped
1 red chilli, chopped
425 ml/15 fl oz Fresh Vegetable Stock
  (see page 16)
150 ml/5 fl oz milk
shredded leek, to garnish

NUTRITION
Calories *167*; Sugars *5 g*; Protein *4 g*;
Carbohydrate *8 g*; Fat *13 g*; Saturates *3 g*

 very easy

 15 mins

10 mins

🌼 COOK'S TIP

If serving chilled, transfer from the food processor to a bowl, stir in the vegetable stock and milk, cover and chill in the refrigerator for at least 4 hours.

This is a classic creamy soup made from potatoes and leeks. To achieve the delicate pale colour, be sure to use only the white parts of the leeks.

Vichyssoise

SERVES 6

3 large leeks
3 tbsp butter or margarine
1 onion, thinly sliced
500 g/1 lb 2 oz potatoes, chopped
850 ml/1½ pints Fresh Vegetable Stock
   (see page 16)
2 tsp lemon juice
pinch of ground nutmeg
¼ tsp ground coriander
1 bay leaf
1 egg yolk
150 ml/5 fl oz single cream
salt and pepper
freshly snipped chives, to garnish

1 Trim the leeks and remove most of the green parts. Slice the white parts of the leeks very finely.

2 Melt the butter or margarine in a saucepan. Add the leeks and onion and fry, stirring occasionally, for about 5 minutes without browning.

3 Add the potatoes, stock, lemon juice, nutmeg, coriander and bay leaf to the pan, season to taste with salt and pepper and bring to the boil. Cover and simmer for about 30 minutes, until all the vegetables are very soft.

4 Cool the soup a little, remove and discard the bay leaf and then press through a sieve or process in a food processor or blender until smooth. Pour into a clean saucepan.

5 Blend the egg yolk into the cream, add a little of the soup to the mixture and then whisk it all back into the soup and reheat gently, without boiling. Adjust the seasoning to taste. Leave to cool and then chill thoroughly in the refrigerator.

6 Serve the soup sprinkled with freshly snipped chives.

NUTRITION

Calories 208; Sugars 5 g; Protein 5 g;
Carbohydrate 20 g; Fat 12 g; Saturates 6 g

 very easy
 10 mins
10 mins
40 mins

This is a really filling soup, which is best served before a light main course. It is easy to prepare and filled with flavour.

Vegetable *and* Corn Chowder

1 Heat the oil in a large saucepan. Add the onion, red pepper, garlic and potatoes and sauté over a low heat, stirring frequently, for 2–3 minutes.

2 Stir in the flour and cook, stirring, for 30 seconds. Gradually stir in the milk and stock.

3 Add the broccoli and sweetcorn. Bring the mixture to the boil, stirring constantly, then reduce the heat and simmer for about 20 minutes, or until all the vegetables are tender.

4 Stir in 50 g/1¾ oz of the cheese until it melts.

5 Season to taste, then spoon the chowder into a warm soup tureen. Garnish with the remaining cheese and the coriander and serve.

SERVES 4

1 tbsp vegetable oil
1 red onion, diced
1 red pepper, halved, deseeded and diced
3 garlic cloves, crushed
300 g/10½ oz potatoes, diced
2 tbsp plain flour
600 ml/1 pint milk
300 ml/10 fl oz Fresh Vegetable Stock (see page 16)
50 g/1¾ oz broccoli florets
300 g/10½ oz canned sweetcorn, drained
75 g/2¾ oz Cheddar cheese, grated
salt and pepper
1 tbsp chopped fresh coriander, to garnish

NUTRITION
Calories *378*; Sugars *20 g*; Protein *16 g*;
Carbohydrate *52 g*; Fat *13 g*; Saturates *6 g*

 moderate

15 mins

20 mins

 COOK'S TIP

Vegetarian cheeses are made with rennets of non-animal origin, using microbial or fungal enzymes.

Dhal is a delicious Indian lentil dish. This soup is a variation on the theme – it is made with red lentils and spiced with curry powder.

Curried Lentil Soup

SERVES 4

25 g/1 oz butter
2 garlic cloves, crushed
1 onion, chopped
¹/₂ tsp turmeric
1 tsp garam masala
¹/₄ tsp chilli powder
1 tsp ground cumin
1 kg/2 lb 4 oz canned chopped
   tomatoes, drained
175 g/6 oz red lentils, washed
2 tsp lemon juice
600 ml/1 pint Fresh Vegetable Stock
   (see page 16)
300 ml/10 fl oz coconut milk
salt and pepper
naan bread, to serve

to garnish
chopped coriander
lemon slices

1 Melt the butter in a large saucepan and sauté the crushed garlic and onion for 2–3 minutes, stirring. Add the turmeric, garam masala, chilli powder and ground cumin and cook for a further 30 seconds.

2 Stir in the tomatoes, red lentils, lemon juice, vegetable stock and coconut milk and bring to the boil.

3 Reduce the heat and simmer for 25–30 minutes until the lentils are tender and cooked.

4 Season to taste and spoon the soup into a warm tureen. Garnish with the chopped coriander and lemon slices and serve with warm naan bread.

NUTRITION

Calories 284; Sugars 13 g; Protein 16 g; Carbohydrate 38 g; Fat 9 g; Saturates 5 g

   moderate
   10 mins
   35 mins

🍲 **COOK'S TIP**

You can buy cans of coconut milk from supermarkets and delicatessens. It can also be made by grating creamed coconut, which comes in the form of a solid bar, and mixing it with water.

Beans feature widely in Mexican cooking, and here pinto beans are used to give an interesting texture. Pinto beans require soaking overnight.

Bean Soup

1 Drain the beans and place in a saucepan with the water. Bring to the boil and boil vigorously for 10 minutes. Lower the heat, cover and simmer for 2 hours, or until the beans are tender.

2 Add the carrots, onion, garlic, chilli and stock and bring back to the boil. Cover and simmer for a further 30 minutes, until very tender.

3 Remove half the beans and vegetables with the cooking juices and press through a strainer or process in a food processor or blender until smooth.

4 Return the bean purée to the saucepan and add the tomatoes and celery. Simmer for 10–15 minutes, or until the celery is just tender, adding a little more stock or water if necessary.

5 Meanwhile, prepare the croûtons. Dice the bread. Heat the oil with the garlic in a small frying pan and fry the croûtons until golden brown. Drain on kitchen paper.

6 Season the soup and stir in the chopped coriander, if using. Transfer to a warm tureen and serve immediately with the croûtons.

SERVES 4

175 g/6 oz pinto beans, soaked overnight in water
1.25 litres/2¼ pints water
175–225 g/6–8 oz carrots, chopped finely
1 large onion, chopped finely
2–3 garlic cloves, crushed
½–1 chilli, deseeded and chopped finely
1 litre /1¾ pints Fresh Vegetable Stock
2 tomatoes, peeled and chopped finely
2 celery sticks, sliced very thinly
salt and pepper
1 tbsp chopped coriander (optional)

croûtons

3 slices white bread, crusts removed
oil, for deep-frying
1–2 garlic cloves, crushed

NUTRITION

Calories *188*; Sugars *9 g*; Protein *13 g*; Carbohydrate *33 g*; Fat *1 g*; Saturates *0.3 g*

 easy

 8 hrs/20 mins

3 hrs

🥄 COOK'S TIP

Pinto beans are widely available, but if you cannot find them or you wish to vary the recipe, you can use cannellini beans or black-eyed beans as an alternative.

A thick and hearty soup, nourishing and substantial enough to serve as a main meal with warmed wholemeal bread.

Indian Bean Soup

S E R V E S 4

4 tbsp vegetable ghee or vegetable oil
2 onions, peeled and chopped
225 g/8 oz potato, cut into chunks
225 g/8 oz parsnip, cut into chunks
225 g/8 oz turnip or swede, cut into chunks
2 celery sticks, sliced
2 courgettes, sliced
1 green pepper, deseeded and cut into 1-cm/½-inch pieces
2 garlic cloves, crushed
2 tsp ground coriander
1 tbsp paprika
1 tbsp mild curry paste
1.2 litres/2 pints Fresh Vegetable Stock (see page 16)
salt
400 g/14 oz canned black-eye beans, drained and rinsed
chopped fresh coriander, to garnish (optional)

1 Heat the ghee or oil in a saucepan, add all the prepared vegetables, except the courgettes and green pepper, and cook over a moderate heat, stirring frequently, for 5 minutes. Add the garlic, ground coriander, paprika and curry paste and cook, stirring constantly, for 1 minute.

2 Stir in the stock and season with salt to taste. Bring to the boil, cover and simmer over a low heat, stirring occasionally, for 25 minutes.

3 Stir in the black-eye beans, sliced courgettes and green pepper, then replace the lid and continue cooking for a further 15 minutes, or until all the vegetables are tender.

4 Process 300 ml/10 fl oz of the soup mixture (about 2 ladlefuls) in a food processor or blender. Return the puréed mixture to the soup in the saucepan and reheat until piping hot. Sprinkle with chopped coriander if using, and serve hot.

N U T R I T I O N
Calories 237; Sugars 9 g; Protein 9 g; Carbohydrate 33 g; Fat 9 g; Saturates 1 g

  very easy
  15 mins
     50 mins

Make the most of home-grown herbs to create this wonderfully creamy soup with its marvellous garden-fresh fragrance.

Cream Cheese *and* Herb Soup

1 Melt the butter or margarine in a large, heavy-based saucepan. Add the onions and fry over a medium heat for 2 minutes, then cover and turn the heat to low. Continue to cook the onions for 5 minutes, then remove the lid.

2 Add the vegetable stock and herbs to the saucepan. Bring to the boil over a moderate heat. Lower the heat, cover and simmer gently for 20 minutes.

3 Remove the saucepan from the heat. Transfer the soup to a food processor or blender and process for about 15 seconds, until smooth. Alternatively, press it through a sieve with the back of a wooden spoon. Return the soup to the saucepan.

4 Reserve a little of the cheese for garnish. Spoon the remaining cheese into the soup and whisk until it has melted and is incorporated.

5 Mix the cornflour with the milk to a paste, then stir the mixture into the soup. Heat, stirring constantly, until thickened and smooth.

6 Pour the soup into warmed individual bowls. Spoon some of the reserved cheese into each bowl and garnish with chives. Serve at once.

SERVES 4

25 g/1 oz butter or margarine
2 onions, chopped
850 ml/1½ pints Fresh Vegetable Stock (see page 16)
25 g/1 oz coarsely chopped mixed fresh herbs, such as parsley, chives, thyme, basil and oregano
200 g/7 oz full-fat soft cheese
1 tbsp cornflour
1 tbsp milk
chopped chives, to garnish

NUTRITION
Calories 275; Sugars 5 g; Protein 0 g; Carbohydrate 14 g; Fat 22 g; Saturates 11 g

 very easy
 15 mins
 35 mins

Starters

With so many fresh ingredients readily available, it is very easy to create some deliciously different starters to make the perfect introduction to a vegetarian meal. The ideas in this chapter are an inspiration to cook and a treat to eat, and they give an edge to the appetite that makes the main course even more enjoyable. When choosing a starter, make sure that you provide a good balance of flavours, colours and textures that offer variety and contrast. Balance the nature of the recipes too – a rich main course is best preceded by a light starter, which is just enough to interest the palate and stimulate the tastebuds.

Anyone who loves garlic will adore this dip – it is very potent! Serve it at a barbecue and dip raw vegetables or chunks of French bread into it.

Heavenly Garlic Dip

SERVES 4

2 garlic bulbs
6 tbsp olive oil
1 small onion, chopped finely
2 tbsp lemon juice
3 tbsp tahini
2 tbsp chopped fresh parsley
salt and pepper

to serve
fresh vegetable crudités
French bread or warmed pitta breads

1 Separate the garlic bulbs into individual cloves. Place them on a baking tray and roast in a preheated oven, 200°C/400°F/Gas Mark 6, for about 8–10 minutes. Set them aside to cool for a few minutes. When they are cool enough to handle, peel the garlic cloves and then finely chop.

2 Heat the olive oil in a saucepan or frying pan and add the garlic and onion. Fry over a low heat, stirring occasionally, for 8–10 minutes, until softened. Remove the pan from the heat.

3 Mix in the lemon juice, tahini and parsley. Season to taste with salt and pepper. Transfer the dip to a small heatproof bowl and keep warm at one side of the barbecue.

4 Serve with fresh vegetable crudités, or with chunks of French bread or warm pitta breads.

NUTRITION
Calories 344; Sugars 2 g; Protein 6 g;
Carbohydrate 3 g; Fat 34 g; Saturates 5 g

 very easy
15 mins
20 mins

COOK'S TIP

If you come across smoked garlic, use it in this recipe – it tastes wonderful. There is no need to roast the smoked garlic, so omit the first step. This dip can also be used to baste vegetarian burgers.

This tasty dip is very easy to make. It is perfect to have at barbecues, as it gives your guests something to nibble while they are waiting.

Buttered Nut *and* Lentil Dip

1 Melt half the butter in a saucepan, add the onion and fry over a medium heat, stirring frequently, until it is golden brown in colour.

2 Add the lentils and vegetable stock. Bring to the boil, then reduce the heat and simmer gently, uncovered, for about 25–30 minutes, until the lentils are tender. Drain well.

3 Melt the remaining butter in a small frying pan. Add the almonds and pine kernels and fry them over a low heat, stirring frequently, until golden brown. Remove the pan from the heat.

4 Put the lentils, the almonds and the pine kernels into a food processor or blender, together with any butter remaining in the frying pan. Add the ground coriander, cumin, ginger and fresh coriander. Process for about 15–20 seconds, until the mixture is smooth. Alternatively, press the lentils through a sieve with the back of a wooden spoon to purée them and then mix with the chopped finely nuts, spices and herbs.

5 Season the dip with salt and pepper and garnish with fresh coriander sprigs. Serve with fresh vegetable crudités and bread sticks.

SERVES 4

55 g/2 oz butter
1 small onion, chopped
90 g/3¼ oz red lentils, washed
300 ml/10 fl oz Fresh Vegetable Stock
    (see page 16)
55 g/2 oz blanched almonds
55 g/2 oz pine kernels
½ tsp ground coriander
½ tsp ground cumin
½ tsp grated root ginger
1 tsp chopped fresh coriander
salt and pepper
fresh coriander sprigs, to garnish

to serve
fresh vegetable crudités
bread sticks

NUTRITION
Calories *395*; Sugars *4 g*; Protein *12 g*;
Carbohydrate *18 g*; Fat *31 g*; Saturates *10 g*

easy

5–10 mins

1 hr

🧑‍🍳 COOK'S TIP

Green or brown lentils can be used, but they will take longer to cook than red lentils. If you wish, substitute peanuts for the almonds. Ground ginger can be used instead of fresh – substitute ½ teaspoon and add it with the other spices.

This wonderful soft cheese pâté is fragrant with the aroma of fresh herbs and garlic. Serve with triangles of Melba toast for a perfect starter.

Cheese, Garlic *and* Herb Pâté

SERVES 4

15 g/½ oz butter
1 garlic clove, crushed
3 spring onions, chopped finely
125 g/4½ oz full-fat soft cheese
2 tbsp chopped mixed fresh herbs, such as parsley, chives, marjoram, oregano and basil
175 g/6 oz finely grated mature Cheddar cheese
pepper
4–6 slices of white bread from a medium-cut sliced loaf

to garnish
ground paprika
herb sprigs

to serve
mixed salad leaves
cherry tomatoes

1 Melt the butter in a small frying pan and gently fry the garlic and spring onions together for 3–4 minutes, until softened. Allow to cool.

2 Beat the soft cheese in a large mixing bowl until smooth, then add the garlic and spring onions. Stir in the chopped mixed fresh herbs, mixing well.

3 Add the Cheddar and work the mixture together to form a stiff paste. Cover and chill until ready to serve.

4 To make the Melba toast, toast the slices of bread on both sides, and then cut off the crusts. Using a sharp bread knife, cut through the slices horizontally to make very thin slices. Cut into triangles and then lightly grill the untoasted sides until golden.

5 Arrange the mixed salad leaves on 4 serving plates with the cherry tomatoes. Pile the cheese pâté on top and sprinkle with a little paprika. Garnish with fresh herbs sprigs and serve with the Melba toast.

NUTRITION
Calories 392; Sugars 1 g; Protein 17 g; Carbohydrate 18 g; Fat 28 g; Saturates 18 g

 very easy
 20 mins
10 mins

Red lentils are used in this spicy recipe for speed as they do not require pre-soaking. If you use other lentils, soak and pre-cook them first.

Lentil Pâté

1 Heat the vegetable oil in a large saucepan and sauté the onion and garlic for 2–3 minutes, stirring. Add the spices and cook for a further 30 seconds. Stir in the vegetable stock and lentils and bring the mixture to the boil. Reduce the heat and simmer for 20 minutes until the lentils are cooked and softened. Remove the pan from the heat and drain off any excess moisture.

2 Put the mixture in a food processor and add the egg, milk, mango chutney and parsley. Blend until smooth.

3 Grease and line the base of a 450 g/ 1 lb loaf tin and spoon the mixture into the tin. Cover and cook in a preheated oven, 200°C/400°F/Gas Mark 6, for 40–45 minutes or until firm.

4 Allow the pâté to cool in the tin for 20 minutes, then transfer to the refrigerator to cool completely. Slice the pâté and garnish with parsley sprigs. Serve with salad leaves and warm toast.

SERVES 4

1 tbsp vegetable oil, plus extra for greasing
1 onion, chopped
2 garlic cloves, crushed
1 tsp garam masala
$\frac{1}{2}$ tsp ground coriander
850 ml/1$\frac{1}{2}$ pints Fresh Vegetable Stock
   (see page 16)
175 g/6 oz red lentils, washed
1 small egg
2 tbsp milk
2 tbsp mango chutney
2 tbsp chopped fresh parsley
fresh parsley sprigs, to garnish

to serve
salad leaves
warm toast

COOK'S TIP

Use other spices, such as chilli powder or Chinese five-spice powder, to flavour the pâté and add tomato relish or chilli relish instead of the mango chutney, if you prefer.

NUTRITION
Calories *267*; Sugars *12 g*; Protein *14 g*; Carbohydrate *37 g*; Fat *8 g*; Saturates *1 g*

   easy

   40 mins

   1 hr 15 mins

This is a really quick starter to prepare if canned beans are used. Choose a wide variety of beans for colour and flavour.

Mixed Bean Pâté

S E R V E S 4

400 g/14 oz canned mixed beans, drained
2 tbsp olive oil
juice of 1 lemon
2 garlic cloves, crushed
1 tbsp chopped fresh coriander
2 spring onions, chopped
salt and pepper
shredded spring onions, to garnish

1 Rinse the beans thoroughly under cold running water and drain well.

2 Transfer the beans to a food processor or blender and process until smooth. Alternatively, place the beans in a bowl and mash thoroughly by hand with a fork or potato masher.

3 Add the olive oil, lemon juice, garlic, coriander and spring onions and blend until fairly smooth. Season with salt and pepper to taste.

4 Transfer the pâté to a serving bowl, cover and chill in the refrigerator for at least 30 minutes.

5 Garnish with shredded spring onions and serve.

N U T R I T I O N
Calories 126; Sugars 3 g; Protein 5 g;
Carbohydrate 13 g; Fat 6 g; Saturates 1 g

 very easy

 45 mins

 0 mins

If you use frozen spinach, it only needs to be thawed and drained before being mixed with the cheeses and seasonings.

Spinach Filo Baskets

1 If using fresh spinach, cook it in the minimum of boiling salted water for 3–4 minutes, until tender. Drain very thoroughly, using a potato masher to remove excess liquid, then chop and put into a bowl. If using frozen spinach, simply drain and chop.

2 Add the spring onions or onion, garlic, cheeses, allspice, egg yolk and seasoning, and mix well.

3 Grease 2 individual Yorkshire pudding tins, or alternatively use ovenproof dishes or tins about 12-cm/5-inches in diameter, and 4-cm/1½-inches deep. Cut the filo pastry sheets in half to make 8 pieces and brush each piece lightly with melted butter.

4 Place 1 piece of filo pastry in a tin or dish and then cover with a second piece at right angles to the first. Add 2 more pieces at right angles, so that all the corners are in different places. Line the other tin in the same way.

5 Spoon the spinach mixture into the 'baskets' and cook in a preheated oven, 180°C/350°F/Gas Mark 4, for about 20 minutes, or until the pastry is golden brown. Garnish with a spring onion tassel and serve hot or cold.

SERVES 4

125 g/4½ oz fresh leaf spinach, washed and chopped roughly, or 90 g/3 oz thawed frozen spinach
2–4 spring onions, trimmed and chopped, or 1 tbsp finely chopped onion
1 garlic clove, crushed
2 tbsp grated Parmesan cheese
90 g/3¼ oz grated mature Cheddar cheese
pinch of ground allspice
1 egg yolk
4 sheets filo pastry
25 g/1 oz butter, melted
salt and pepper
2 spring onions, to garnish

COOK'S TIP

Make the spring onion tassels about 30 minutes before required. Trim off the root end and cut to a length of 5–7 cm/2–3 inches. Make a series of cuts from the green end to within 2-cm/¾-inch of the other end. Place in a bowl of iced water to open out. Drain well before use.

NUTRITION

Calories 533; Sugars 3 g; Protein 24 g; Carbohydrate 26 g; Fat 38 g; Saturates 22 g

 moderate

 30 mins

30 mins

25 mins

These crisp-baked bread cases, filled with sliced tomatoes, feta cheese, black olives and quail's eggs, are quick to make and taste delicious.

Feta Cheese Tartlets

S E R V E S 4

8 slices bread from a medium-cut large loaf
125 g/4½ oz butter, melted
125 g/4½ oz feta cheese, cut into small cubes
4 cherry tomatoes, cut into wedges
8 pitted black or green olives, halved
8 quail's eggs, hard-boiled
2 tbsp olive oil
1 tbsp wine vinegar
1 tsp wholegrain mustard
pinch of caster sugar
salt and pepper
fresh parsley sprigs, to garnish

1 Remove the crusts from the bread. Trim the bread into squares and flatten each piece with a rolling pin.

2 Brush the bread squares with melted butter, and then arrange them in bun or muffin tins. Press a piece of crumpled foil into each bread case to secure in place. Bake the cases in a preheated oven, 190°C/375°F/Gas Mark 5, for 10 minutes, or until crisp and browned.

3 Meanwhile, mix together the feta cheese, tomatoes and olives. Shell the eggs and quarter them. Mix together the olive oil, vinegar, mustard and sugar. Season to taste with salt and pepper.

4 Remove the bread cases from the oven and discard the foil. Leave to cool.

5 Just before serving, fill the bread cases with the cheese and tomato mixture. Arrange the eggs on top and spoon over the dressing. Garnish with parsley sprigs.

N U T R I T I O N
Calories 570; Sugars 3 g; Protein 14 g;
Carbohydrate 36 g; Fat 42 g; Saturates 23 g

 very easy

 30 mins

10 mins

Hummus is especially good spread on these garlic toasts for a delicious starter or as part of a light lunch.

Hummus Toasts *with* Olives

1 To make the hummus, firstly drain the chickpeas, reserving a little of the liquid. Put the chickpeas and liquid in a food processor and blend, gradually adding the reserved liquid and lemon juice. Blend well after each addition until smooth.

2 Stir in the tahini and all but 1 teaspoon of the olive oil. Add the garlic, season to taste and blend again until smooth.

3 Spoon the hummus into a serving dish. Drizzle the remaining olive oil over the top, garnish with chopped coriander and olives. Leave to chill in the refrigerator while preparing the toasts.

4 Lay the slices of ciabatta on a grill rack in a single layer.

5 Mix the garlic, coriander and olive oil together and drizzle over the bread slices. Cook under a hot grill for 2–3 minutes until golden brown, turning once. Serve hot with the hummus.

SERVES 4

400 g/14 oz canned chickpeas
juice of 1 large lemon
6 tbsp tahini
2 tbsp olive oil
2 garlic cloves, crushed
salt and pepper
1 ciabatta loaf, sliced
2 garlic cloves, crushed
1 tbsp chopped fresh coriander
4 tbsp olive oil

to garnish
chopped fresh coriander
black olives

NUTRITION
Calories 731; Sugars 2 g; Protein 22 g;
Carbohydrate 39 g; Fat 55 g; Saturates 8 g

 moderate

 15 mins

15 mins

2-3 mins

This is a well-known method of cooking vegetables and is perfect with shallots or onions, served with a crisp salad.

Onions *à la* Grecque

S E R V E S 4

450 g/1 lb shallots
3 tbsp olive oil
3 tbsp clear honey
2 tbsp garlic wine vinegar
3 tbsp dry white wine
1 tbsp tomato purée
2 celery sticks, sliced
2 tomatoes, deseeded and chopped
salt and pepper
chopped celery leaves, to garnish

1 Peel the shallots. Heat the oil in a large saucepan, add the shallots and cook, stirring, for 3–5 minutes, or until they begin to brown.

2 Add the honey and cook over a high heat for a further 30 seconds, then add the garlic wine vinegar and dry white wine, stirring well.

3 Stir in the tomato purée, the celery and the tomatoes, and bring the mixture to the boil. Cook over a high heat for 5–6 minutes. Season to taste and leave to cool slightly.

4 Garnish with chopped celery leaves and serve warm. Alternatively chill in the refrigerator before serving.

N U T R I T I O N
Calories *200*; Sugars *26 g*; Protein *2 g*;
Carbohydrate *28 g*; Fat *9 g*; Saturates *1 g*

 very easy
 10 mins
 15 mins

Make this Mexican-style salsa to perk up jaded palates. Its lively flavours really get the tastebuds going. Serve with hot tortilla chips.

Fiery Salsa

1 Remove and discard the stem and seeds from 1 fresh red chilli. Chop the flesh very finely and place in a large mixing bowl.

2 Use the other red chilli to make a 'flower' for the garnish. Using a small, sharp knife, slice the remaining chilli from the stem to the tip several times without removing the stem, so the slices remain attached. Place in a bowl of iced water so that the 'petals' open out.

3 Add the lime juice to the chilli in the mixing bowl. Halve, stone and peel the avocados. Add the flesh to the mixing bowl and mash thoroughly with a fork. The salsa should be slightly chunky. (The lime or lemon juice prevents the avocado from turning brown.)

4 Finely chop the cucumber and tomatoes and add to the avocado mixture with the crushed garlic.

5 Stir in the Tabasco sauce and season with salt and pepper. Transfer the salsa to a serving bowl. Garnish with slices of lime and the chilli flower.

6 Put the bowl on a large plate, surround with tortilla chips and serve. Do not keep this dip standing for long or it will discolour.

SERVES 4

2 small fresh red chillies
1 tbsp lime or lemon juice
2 large ripe avocados
5-cm/2-inch piece of cucumber
2 tomatoes, peeled
1 small garlic clove, crushed
dash of Tabasco sauce
salt and pepper
lime or lemon slices, to garnish
tortilla chips, to serve

NUTRITION
Calories 328; Sugars 2 g; Protein 4 g;
Carbohydrate 21 g; Fat 26 g; Saturates 5 g

   easy

   30 mins

   0 mins

Thin slices of vegetables
are wrapped in pastry and
deep-fried until crisp.
Spring roll wrappers are
available fresh or frozen.

Spring Rolls

MAKES 12

5 Chinese dried mushrooms
  (if unavailable, use open-cup mushrooms)
2 tbsp vegetable oil
1 large carrot, cut into julienne strips
55 g/2 oz canned bamboo shoots, cut into
  julienne strips
2 spring onions, chopped
55 g/2 oz Chinese leaves, shredded
225 g/8 oz beansprouts
1 tbsp soy sauce
12 spring roll wrappers
1 egg, beaten
vegetable oil, for deep-frying
salt

1 Place the dried mushrooms in a small bowl and cover with warm water. Leave to soak for 20–25 minutes.

2 Drain the mushrooms and squeeze out the excess water. Remove the tough centres and slice the mushroom caps thinly.

3 Heat the 2 tablespoons of oil in a wok. Add the mushrooms, carrot and bamboo shoots and stir-fry for 2 minutes. Add the spring onions, Chinese leaves, beansprouts and soy sauce. Season with salt and stir-fry for 2 minutes. Leave to cool.

4 Divide the mixture into 12 equal portions and place one portion on the edge of each spring roll wrapper. Fold in the sides and roll each one up, brushing the join with a little beaten egg to seal.

5 Deep-fry the spring rolls in batches in hot oil in a wok or large saucepan for 4–5 minutes, or until golden and crispy. Take care that the oil is not too hot or the spring rolls will brown on the outside before cooking on the inside. Remove and drain on kitchen paper. Keep each batch warm while the others are being cooked. Serve at once.

NUTRITION
Calories 186; Sugars 2 g; Protein 4 g;
Carbohydrate 18 g; Fat 11 g; Saturates 1 g

easy

45 mins

25–30 mins

Crispy coated vegetables and tofu, accompanied by a sweet, spicy dip, give a real taste of the Orient in this Japanese-style dish.

Tofu Tempura

1 Slice the courgettes and carrots in half lengthways. Trim the corn. Trim the leeks at both ends. Cut the aubergines into quarters lengthways. Cut the tofu into 2.5-cm/1-inch cubes.

2 To make the batter, mix the egg yolks with the water. Sift in 175 g/6 oz of the flour and beat with a balloon whisk to form a thick batter. Don't worry if there are any lumps. Heat the oil for deep-frying to 180°C/350°F or until a cube of bread browns in 30 seconds.

3 Place the remaining flour on a large plate and toss the vegetables and tofu until lightly coated.

4 Dip the tofu in the batter and deep-fry for 2–3 minutes, until lightly golden. Drain on kitchen paper and keep warm.

5 Dip the vegetables in the batter and deep-fry, a few at a time, for 3–4 minutes, until golden. Drain and place on a warmed serving plate.

6 To make the dipping sauce, mix all the ingredients together. Serve with the vegetables and tofu, accompanied with noodles and garnished with julienne strips of vegetables.

SERVES 4

125 g/4¹/₂ oz baby courgettes
125 g/4¹/₂ oz baby carrots
125 g/4¹/₂ oz baby corn cobs
125 g/4¹/₂ oz baby leeks
2 baby aubergines
225 g/8 oz tofu
vegetable oil, for deep-frying
mixed vegetable julienne strips, to garnish
cooked noodles, to serve

batter
2 egg yolks
300 ml/ 10 fl oz water
225 g/8 oz plain flour

dipping sauce
5 tbsp mirin or dry sherry
5 tbsp Japanese soy sauce
2 tsp clear honey
1 garlic clove, crushed
1 tsp grated fresh root ginger

NUTRITION
Calories 582; Sugars 10 g; Protein 16 g;
Carbohydrate 65 g; Fat 27 g; Saturates 4 g

 very easy
 15 mins
15 mins
20 mins

These small bhajis are often served as accompaniments to a main meal, but they are delicious as a starter with a small salad and yogurt sauce.

Mixed Bhajis

SERVES 4

bhajis
175 g/6 oz gram flour
1 tsp bicarbonate of soda
2 tsp ground coriander
1 tsp garam masala
1½ tsp turmeric
1½ tsp chilli powder
2 tbsp chopped fresh coriander
1 small onion, halved and sliced
1 small leek, sliced
100 g/3½ oz cooked cauliflower
9–12 tbsp cold water
salt and pepper
vegetable oil, for deep-frying

sauce
150 ml/5 fl oz natural yogurt
2 tbsp chopped fresh mint
½ tsp turmeric
1 garlic clove, crushed
fresh mint sprigs, to garnish

1 Sift the flour, bicarbonate of soda and salt to taste into a mixing bowl and add the spices and fresh coriander. Mix together thoroughly.

2 Divide the mixture into 3 and place in separate bowls. Stir the onion into one bowl, the leek into another and the cauliflower into the third bowl. Add 3–4 tablespoons of water to each bowl and mix each to form a smooth paste.

3 Heat the vegetable oil in a deep fryer to 180°C/350°F or until a cube of bread browns in 30 seconds. Using 2 dessert spoons, form the mixture into rounds and cook each in the oil for 3–4 minutes, until browned.

4 Remove the bhajis with a slotted spoon, drain well on absorbent kitchen paper and keep warm in the oven while cooking the remainder.

5 Mix the sauce ingredients together, garnish with mint sprigs and serve with the warm bhajis.

NUTRITION
Calories *414*; Sugars *7 g*; Protein *9 g*;
Carbohydrate *38 g*; Fat *26 g*; Saturates *3 g*

easy
25 mins
20 mins

This is a very versatile dish that will go with almost anything and can be served warm or cold. It is perfect as a starter for a dinner party.

Hyderabad Pickles

1 Dry-fry the ground coriander, cumin, coconut, sesame seeds and mustard and onion seeds in a frying pan until lightly coloured and the spices release their aroma. Grind in a pestle and mortar or food processor and set aside.

2 Heat the oil in a frying pan and fry the onions until golden. Reduce the heat and add the ginger, garlic, turmeric, chilli powder and salt, stirring. Leave to cool, then grind this mixture to form a paste.

3 Make 4 cuts across each aubergine half. Blend the spices with the onion paste. Spoon this mixture into the slits in the aubergines.

4 In a bowl, mix the tamarind paste and 3 tablespoons of water to make a fine paste and set aside.

5 For the baghaar, fry the onion and mustard seeds, cumin seeds and red chillies in the oil. Reduce the heat, place the aubergines in the baghaar and stir gently. Stir in the tamarind paste and the 250 ml/9 fl oz water and cook over a medium heat for 15–20 minutes. Add the coriander leaves and green chilli.

6 When cool, transfer to a serving dish and serve garnished with the hard-boiled eggs.

SERVES 4

2 tsp ground coriander
2 tsp ground cumin
2 tsp desiccated coconut
2 tsp sesame seeds
1 tsp mixed mustard and onion seeds
300 ml/10 fl oz vegetable oil
3 medium onions, sliced
1 tsp finely chopped fresh root ginger
1 tsp crushed garlic
½ tsp turmeric
1½ tsp chilli powder
1½ tsp salt
3 medium aubergines, halved lengthways
1 tbsp tamarind paste
3 hard-boiled eggs, halved, to garnish

baghaar
1 tsp mixed onion and mustard seeds
1 tsp cumin seeds
4 dried red chillies
150 ml/5 fl oz vegetable oil
coriander leaves
1 green chilli, chopped finely

NUTRITION
Calories *732*; Sugars *6 g*; Protein *6 g*; Carbohydrate *8 g*; Fat *75 g*; Saturates *10 g*

 easy

 30 mins

 30 mins

Whole mushrooms are dunked in a spiced garlicky batter and deep-fried until golden. They are at their most delicious served piping hot.

Garlicky Mushroom Pakoras

SERVES 4

175 g/6 oz gram flour
½ tsp salt
¼ tsp baking powder
1 tsp cumin seeds
½–1 tsp chilli powder
200 ml/7 fl oz water
2 garlic cloves, crushed
1 small onion, chopped finely
vegetable oil, for deep-frying
500 g/1 lb 2 oz button mushrooms, trimmed and wiped

to garnish
lemon wedges
coriander sprigs

1 Put the gram flour, salt, baking powder, cumin seeds and chilli powder into a bowl and mix well together. Make a well in the centre of the mixture and gradually stir in the water, mixing thoroughly to form a batter.

2 Stir the crushed garlic and the chopped onion into the batter and leave the mixture to infuse for 10 minutes. One-third fill a deep-fat fryer or pan with vegetable oil and heat to 180°C/350°F or until a cube of bread browns in 30 seconds. Lower the basket into the hot oil.

3 Meanwhile, mix the mushrooms into the batter, stirring to coat. Remove a few at a time and place them into the hot oil. Fry for about 2 minutes, or until golden brown.

4 Remove the mushrooms from the pan with a slotted spoon and drain on kitchen paper while you are cooking the remainder in the same way.

5 Serve hot, sprinkled with coarse salt and garnished with lemon wedges and coriander sprigs.

NUTRITION
Calories 297; Sugars 3 g; Protein 5 g;
Carbohydrate 24 g; Fat 21 g; Saturates 2 g

easy
20 mins
10–15 mins

🌀 **COOK'S TIP**

Gram flour, also known as besan flour, is a pale yellow flour made from chickpeas. It is now readily available from larger supermarkets, as well as Indian food shops and some ethnic delicatessens.

Samosas, which are a sort of Indian Cornish pasty, make excellent snacks. In India, they are popular snacks at roadside stalls.

Samosas

1 Sift the flour and salt into a bowl. Add the butter and rub into the flour until the mixture resembles fine breadcrumbs.

2 Pour in the water and mix with a fork to form a dough. Pat it into a ball and knead for 5 minutes, or until smooth. Cover and leave to rise in a warm place.

3 To make the filling, mash the boiled potatoes gently and mix with the ginger, garlic, white cumin seeds, onion and mustard seeds, salt, crushed red chillies, lemon juice and green chillies.

4 Break small balls off the dough and roll each out very thinly to form a round. Cut in half, dampen the edges and shape into cones. Fill the cones with a little of the filling, dampen the top and bottom edges of the cones and pinch together to seal. Set aside.

5 Fill a deep saucepan one-third full with oil and heat to 180°C/350°F or until a small cube of bread browns in 30 seconds. Carefully lower the samosas into the oil, a few at a time, and fry for 2–3 minutes, or until golden brown. Remove from the oil and drain thoroughly on kitchen paper. Serve hot or cold.

MAKES 12

pastry
100 g/3½ oz self-raising flour
½ tsp salt
40 g/1½ oz butter, cut into small pieces
4 tbsp water

filling
3 medium potatoes, boiled
1 tsp finely chopped fresh root ginger
1 tsp crushed garlic
½ tsp white cumin seeds
½ tsp mixed onion and mustard seeds
1 tsp salt
½ tsp crushed fresh red chillies
2 tbsp lemon juice
2 small fresh green chillies, chopped finely
ghee or oil, for deep-frying

NUTRITION
Calories 261; Sugars 0.4 g; Protein 2 g; Carbohydrate 13 g; Fat 23 g; Saturates 4 g

⭐⭐⭐　　moderate
🕐　　40 mins
🕐　　15 mins

These puff pastries are ideal with a more formal meal – they only take a short time to prepare but they look really impressive.

Mini Vegetable Puff Pastries

SERVES 4

pastry cases
450 g/1 lb puff pastry
1 egg, beaten

filling
225 g/8 oz sweet potatoes, cubed
100 g/3½ oz baby asparagus spears
2 tbsp butter or margarine
1 leek, sliced
2 small open-cap mushrooms, sliced
1 tsp lime juice
1 tsp chopped fresh thyme
pinch of dried mustard
salt and pepper

1 Cut the pastry into 4 equal pieces. Roll each piece out on a lightly floured work surface to form a 13-cm/ 5-inch square. Place on a dampened baking tray and score a smaller 6-cm/2½ -inch square inside.

2 Brush with the beaten egg and cook in a preheated oven, 200°C/400°F/ Gas Mark 6, for 20 minutes or until risen and golden brown.

3 While the pastry is cooking, start the filling. Cook the sweet potato in boiling water for 15 minutes, then drain. Blanch the asparagus in boiling water for 10 minutes or until tender. Drain and reserve.

4 Remove the pastry squares from the oven. Carefully cut out the central square of pastry, lift it out and reserve.

5 Melt the butter in a saucepan and sauté the leek and mushrooms for 2–3 minutes. Add the lime juice, thyme and mustard, season well and stir in the sweet potatoes and asparagus. Spoon into the pastry cases, top with the reserved pastry squares and serve immediately.

NUTRITION
Calories 210; Sugars 2.3 g; Protein 3.8 g; Carbohydrate 21 g; Fat 13 g; Saturates 1.7 g

easy
15 mins
25 mins

COOK'S TIP

Use a colourful selection of any vegetables you have at hand for this recipe.

These individual soufflés make very impressive starters, but must be cooked just before serving to prevent them from sinking.

Mushroom *and* Garlic Soufflés

1 Lightly grease the inside of 4 150 ml/5 fl oz individual soufflé dishes with a little butter.

2 Melt 25 g/1 oz of the butter in a frying pan. Add the mushrooms, lime juice and garlic and sauté for 2–3 minutes. Remove the mushroom mixture from the frying pan with a slotted spoon and transfer it to a mixing bowl. Stir in the marjoram.

3 Melt the remaining butter in a pan. Add the flour and cook for 1 minute, then remove from the heat. Stir in the milk and return to the heat. Bring to the boil, stirring until thickened.

4 Mix the sauce into the mushroom mixture and beat in the egg yolks.

5 Whisk the egg whites until they form peaks and fold into the mushroom mixture until fully incorporated.

6 Divide the mixture between the prepared soufflé dishes. Place the dishes on a baking tray and cook in a preheated oven, 200°C/400°F/Gas Mark 6, for about 8–10 minutes, or until the soufflés are well risen and cooked through. Serve immediately.

SERVES 4

50 g/1¾ oz butter
75 g/2¾ oz flat mushrooms, chopped
2 tsp lime juice
2 garlic cloves, crushed
2 tbsp chopped fresh marjoram
25 g/1 oz plain flour
225 ml/8 fl oz milk
salt and pepper
2 eggs, separated

NUTRITION
Calories *179*; Sugars *3 g*; Protein *6 g*;
Carbohydrate *8 g*; Fat *14 g*; Saturates *8 g*

 easy
 10 mins
10 mins
20 mins

(😊) COOK'S TIP

Insert a skewer into the centre of the soufflés to test if they are cooked through – it should come out clean. If not, cook for a few minutes longer, but do not overcook or they will become rubbery.

Light Meals

The ability to rustle up a simple snack or a quickly-prepared light meal can be very important in our busy lives. Sometimes we may not feel like eating a full-scale meal, but nevertheless want something appetizing and satisfying. Or if lunch or dinner is going to be served very late, then we may want something to tide us over and stave off those hunger pangs! Whether it is for a sustaining snack to break the day, hearty nibbles to serve with pre-dinner drinks, or an informal lunch or supper party, you'll find a mouthwatering collection of recipes in this chapter.

Roasted vegetables are delicious and attractive. Served on warm muffins with a herb sauce, they are unbeatable.

Vegetable-topped Muffins

S E R V E S   4

1 red onion, cut into 8 wedges
1 aubergine, halved and sliced
1 yellow pepper, halved, deseeded and sliced
1 courgette, sliced
4 tbsp olive oil
1 tbsp garlic vinegar
2 tbsp vermouth
2 garlic cloves, crushed
1 tbsp chopped fresh thyme
2 tsp light brown sugar
4 muffins, halved

sauce
2 tbsp butter
1 tbsp plain flour
150 ml/5 fl oz milk
5 tbsp Fresh Vegetable Stock (see page 16)
85 g/3 oz Cheddar cheese, grated
1 tsp wholegrain mustard
3 tbsp chopped mixed fresh herbs
salt and pepper

N U T R I T I O N
Calories 740; Sugars 27 g; Protein 20 g;
Carbohydrate 67 g; Fat 45 g; Saturates 17 g

   moderate
   1 hr 15 mins
   35 mins

1 Arrange the onion, aubergine, yellow pepper and courgette in a shallow non-metallic dish. Mix together the olive oil, garlic vinegar, vermouth, garlic, thyme and sugar and pour over the vegetables, turning to coat well. Set aside to marinate for 1 hour.

2 Transfer the vegetables to a baking sheet. Roast in a preheated oven, 200°C/400°F/Gas Mark 6, for about 20–25 minutes or until the vegetables have softened.

3 Meanwhile, make the sauce. Melt the butter in a small pan and stir in the flour. Cook, stirring constantly, for 1 minute, then remove from the heat. Gradually stir in the milk and stock and return the pan to the heat. Bring to the boil, stirring constantly until thickened. Stir in the cheese, mustard and mixed herbs and season well.

4 Cut the muffins in half and toast under a preheated grill for 2–3 minutes until golden brown, then transfer to a serving plate. Spoon the roasted vegetables on top of the muffins and pour the sauce over the top. Serve immediately.

This warming Mexican dish consists of tortillas filled with a spicy vegetable mixture and topped with a hot tomato sauce.

Vegetable Enchiladas

1 To make the filling, blanch the spinach in a pan of boiling water for 2 minutes, drain well and chop.

2 Heat the oil in a frying pan and sauté the baby corn, peas, pepper, carrot, leek, garlic and chilli for 3–4 minutes, stirring briskly. Stir in the spinach and season well with salt and pepper to taste.

3 Put all of the sauce ingredients in a saucepan and bring them to the boil, stirring constantly. Continue to cook over a high heat for a further 20 minutes, stirring, until the sauce has thickened and reduced by a third.

4 Spoon a quarter of the filling along the centre of each tortilla. Roll the tortillas around the filling and place in an ovenproof dish, seam-side down.

5 Pour the tomato sauce over the tortillas and sprinkle the grated cheese on top. Cook in a preheated oven, 180°C/350°F/Gas Mark 4, for 20 minutes or until the cheese has melted and browned. Serve immediately.

SERVES 4

4 flour tortillas
75 g/2³/₄ oz Cheddar cheese, grated

filling
75 g/2³/₄ oz spinach
2 tbsp olive oil
8 baby corn cobs, sliced
25 g/1 oz frozen peas, thawed
1 red pepper, halved, deseeded and diced
1 carrot, diced
1 leek, sliced
2 garlic cloves, crushed
1 fresh red chilli, chopped
salt and pepper

sauce
300 ml/10 floz passata
2 shallots, chopped
1 garlic clove, crushed
300 ml/10 fl oz Fresh Vegetable Stock
   (see page 16)
1 tsp caster sugar
1 tsp chilli powder

NUTRITION
Calories *309*; Sugars *14 g*; Protein *12 g*;
Carbohydrate *23 g*; Fat *19 g*; Saturates *8 g*

✪✪✪   moderate
          20 mins
      50 mins

Crêpes are ideal for filling with your favourite ingredients. In this recipe they are packed with a deliciously spicy vegetable filling.

Vegetable Crêpes

SERVES 4

crêpes
100 g/3½ oz plain flour
pinch of salt
1 egg, lightly beaten
300 ml/10 fl oz milk
vegetable oil, for frying

filling
2 tbsp vegetable oil
1 leek, shredded
½ tsp chilli powder
½ tsp ground cumin
55 g/2 oz mangetout
100 g/3½ oz button mushrooms
1 red pepper, halved, deseeded and sliced
4 tbsp cashew nuts, chopped

sauce
2 tbsp margarine
3 tbsp plain flour
150 ml/5 fl oz Vegetable Stock (see page 16)
150 ml/5 fl oz milk
1 tsp Dijon mustard
85 g/3 oz Cheddar cheese, grated
2 tbsp chopped fresh coriander

NUTRITION

Calories 509; Sugars 10 g; Protein 17 g;
Carbohydrate 36 g; Fat 34 g; Saturates 9 g

moderate

15 mins

45 mins

1 For the crêpes, sift the flour and salt into a bowl. Beat in the egg and milk to make a batter.

2 For the filling, heat the oil and cook the leek for 2–3 minutes. Add the remaining ingredients and cook, stirring constantly, for 5 minutes.

3 For the sauce, melt the margarine and add the flour. Cook, stirring, for 1 minute. Remove from the heat, stir in the stock and milk and return to the heat. Bring to the boil, stirring until thickened. Stir in the mustard, half the cheese and the coriander and cook for 1 minute.

4 To make the crêpes, heat 1 tablespoon of oil in a small frying pan. Pour off the oil and add about 2½ tablespoons of the batter. Tilt to cover the base. Cook for 2 minutes, turn and cook the other side for 1 minute. Remove the crêpe and keep warm. Repeat with the remaining batter. Spoon a little of the filling along the centre of each crêpe and roll up. Place in a flameproof dish and pour the sauce on top. Top with cheese and heat under a hot grill for 3–5 minutes or until the cheese melts.

This spicy rice dish is a vegetarian version of the traditional jambalaya. Packed with a variety of vegetables, it is both colourful and nutritious.

Vegetable Jambalaya

1 Cook the rice in a large saucepan of salted boiling water for 20 minutes, or until cooked through. Drain, rinse with boiling water, drain again and set aside.

2 Heat the oil in a heavy-based frying pan and cook the garlic and onion, stirring constantly, for 2–3 minutes. Add the aubergine, pepper, corn, peas and broccoli to the pan and cook, stirring occasionally, for a further 2–3 minutes.

3 Stir in the vegetable stock and the canned tomatoes, tomato purée, creole seasoning and chilli flakes.

4 Season to taste and cook over a low heat for 15–20 minutes, or until the vegetables are tender.

5 Stir the brown rice into the vegetable mixture and cook, mixing well, for 3–4 minutes, or until hot.

6 Transfer the vegetable jambalaya to a warm serving dish and serve at once.

SERVES   4

75 g/2¾ oz brown rice (see Cook's Tip)
2 tbsp olive oil
2 garlic cloves, crushed
1 red onion, cut into 8 wedges
1 aubergine, diced
1 green pepper, halved, deseeded and diced
50 g/1¾ oz baby corn cobs,
   halved lengthways
50 g/1¾ oz frozen peas
100 g/3½ oz small broccoli florets
150 ml/5 fl oz Fresh Vegetable Stock
   (see page 16)
225 g/8 oz canned chopped tomatoes
1 tbsp tomato purée
1 tsp creole seasoning
½ tsp chilli flakes
salt and pepper

NUTRITION
Calories *181*; Sugars *8 g*; Protein *6 g*;
Carbohydrate *25 g*; Fat *7 g*; Saturates *1 g*

      easy

10 mins

50 mins

(😋) **COOK'S TIP**

Use a mixture of different kinds of rice, such as wild or red rice, to add colour and texture to this dish. Cook the rice in advance, following packet instructions, for a speedier recipe.

These spicy vegetable burgers are delicious, especially in a warm bun or roll and served with light oven chips.

Vegetable Burgers *and* Chips

SERVES 4

100 g/3½ oz spinach
2 tbsp olive oil
1 leek, chopped
2 garlic cloves, crushed
100 g/3½ oz mushrooms, chopped
300 g/10½ oz firm tofu, chopped
1 tsp chilli powder
1 tsp curry powder
1 tbsp chopped fresh coriander
75 g/2¾ oz fresh wholemeal breadcrumbs

to serve
burger bap or roll
salad leaves

chips
2 large potatoes
2 tbsp plain flour
1 tsp chilli powder
2 tbsp olive oil

NUTRITION
Calories 461; Sugars 4 g; Protein 18 g;
Carbohydrate 64 g; Fat 17 g; Saturates 2 g

  moderate

1 hr 15 mins

1 hr

1 To make the burgers, cook the spinach in a little boiling water for 2 minutes. Drain thoroughly and pat dry with kitchen paper.

2 Heat 1 tablespoon of the oil in a frying pan and sauté the leek and garlic for 2–3 minutes. Add the remaining ingredients, except the breadcrumbs, and cook for 5–7 minutes until the vegetables have softened. Toss in the spinach and cook for 1 minute.

3 Transfer the mixture to a food processor and process for 30 seconds until almost smooth. Transfer to a bowl, stir in the breadcrumbs, mixing well, and set aside until cool enough to handle. Using floured hands, form the mixture into 4 equal-size burgers. Chill for 30 minutes.

4 To make the chips, cut the potatoes into thin wedges and cook in a pan of boiling water for 10 minutes. Drain and toss in the flour and chilli powder. Lay the chips on a baking sheet and sprinkle with the oil. Cook in a preheated oven, 200°C/400°F/Gas Mark 6, for 30 minutes or until golden.

5 Meanwhile, heat the remaining oil in a frying pan and cook the burgers for 8–10 minutes, turning once. Place in a bap, add some salad leaves and serve with the chips.

This is a very tasty, well-known Middle Eastern dish of small chickpea-based balls, spiced and deep-fried.

Falafel

1 Put the chickpeas, onion, garlic, wholemeal bread, chillies, spices and fresh coriander in a food processor and process for 30 seconds. Stir the mixture and season to taste with salt and pepper.

2 Remove the mixture from the food processor and shape into walnut-sized balls with your hands.

3 Place the beaten egg in a shallow bowl and place the wholemeal breadcrumbs on a plate. First dip the chickpea balls into the egg to coat them thoroughly and then roll them in the breadcrumbs, shaking off any excess.

4 Heat the oil for deep-frying to 180°C/350°F, or until a cube of bread browns in 30 seconds. Fry the falafel, in batches if necessary, for 2–3 minutes, until crisp and browned. Carefully remove them from the oil with a slotted spoon and dry on absorbent kitchen paper.

5 Garnish the falafel with the reserved chopped coriander and serve with a tomato and cucumber salad and lemon wedges.

SERVES 4

675 g/1 lb/8 oz canned chickpeas, drained
1 red onion, chopped
3 garlic cloves, crushed
100 g/3½ oz wholemeal bread
2 small fresh red chillies
1 tsp ground cumin
1 tsp ground coriander
½ tsp turmeric
1 tbsp chopped fresh coriander, plus extra to garnish
1 egg, beaten
100 g/3½ oz wholemeal breadcrumbs
vegetable oil, for deep-frying
salt and pepper

to serve
tomato and cucumber salad
lemon wedges

NUTRITION
Calories 491; Sugars 3 g; Protein 15 g;
Carbohydrate 43 g; Fat 30 g; Saturates 3 g

   easy

25 mins

10–15 mins

These are incredibly simple to make and sure to be popular served as a tempting snack or as an accompaniment to almost any Indian meal.

Potato Fritters *with* Relish

SERVES 4

55 g/2 oz plain wholemeal flour
1/2 tsp ground coriander
1/2 tsp cumin seeds
1/4 tsp chilli powder
1/2 tsp ground turmeric
1/4 tsp salt
1 egg
3 tbsp milk
350 g/12 oz potatoes, peeled
1–2 garlic cloves, crushed
4 spring onions, chopped
55 g/2 oz sweetcorn
vegetable oil, for shallow frying

onion & tomato relish
1 onion, peeled and cut in small dice
225 g/8 oz tomatoes, dices
2 tbsp chopped fresh coriander
2 tbsp chopped fresh mint
2 tbsp lemon juice
1/2 tsp roasted cumin seeds
1/4 tsp salt
pinch of cayenne pepper

NUTRITION
Calories *294*; Sugars *4 g*; Protein *4 g*;
Carbohydrate *18 g*; Fat *24 g*; Saturates *3 g*

easy

30 mins

15 mins

1 First make the relish. Place all the ingredients for the relish in a bowl. Mix together well and leave to stand for at least 15 minutes before serving to allow the flavours to blend.

2 Place the flour in a bowl, stir in the spices and salt and make a well in the centre. Add the egg and milk and mix to form a fairly thick batter.

3 Coarsely grate the potatoes, place them in a sieve and rinse well under cold running water. Drain and squeeze dry, then stir them into the batter with the garlic, spring onions and sweetcorn and mix to combine thoroughly.

4 Heat about 5 mm/1/4 inch of vegetable oil in a large frying pan and add a few tablespoonfuls of the mixture at a time, flattening each one to form a thin cake. Fry over a low heat, turning frequently, for 2–3 minutes, or until golden brown and cooked through.

5 Drain the fritters on absorbent kitchen paper and keep them hot while frying the remaining mixture in the same way. Serve the potato fritters hot with the onion and tomato relish.

These wafer-thin potato crisps are great cooked over a barbecue and served with spicy vegetable kebabs.

Paprika Crisps

1 Using a sharp knife, slice the potatoes very thinly so that they are almost transparent. Pat the potato slices dry with kitchen paper.

2 Heat the oil in a large frying pan and add the paprika, stirring constantly to ensure that the paprika doesn't catch and burn.

3 Add the potato slices to the frying pan and cook them in a single layer for about 5 minutes or until they just begin to curl slightly at the edges.

4 Remove the potato slices from the pan using a slotted spoon and transfer them to kitchen paper to drain thoroughly.

5 Thread the potato slices on to several pre-soaked wooden kebab skewers.

6 Sprinkle the potato slices with a little salt and cook over a medium hot barbecue or under a medium grill, turning frequently, for 10 minutes, until the potato slices begin to go crisp. Sprinkle with a little more salt, if preferred, and serve immediately.

SERVES 4

2 large potatoes
3 tbsp olive oil
½ tsp paprika
salt

NUTRITION

Calories *149*; Sugars *0.6 g*; Protein *2 g*; Carbohydrate *17 g*; Fat *8 g*; Saturates *1 g*

⭐ very easy

🕐 5 mins

🕐 20 mins

 COOK'S TIP

You could use curry powder or any other spice instead of the paprika to flavour the crisps, if you prefer.

VEGETARIAN

Fresh green beans have a wonderful flavour that is hard to beat. If you cannot find fresh beans, use thawed, frozen beans instead.

Mixed Bean Pan-fry

SERVES 4

350 g/12 oz mixed green beans, such as French and broad beans, podded
2 tbsp vegetable oil
2 garlic cloves, crushed
1 red onion, halved and sliced
225 g/8 oz firm marinated tofu, diced
1 tbsp lemon juice
½ tsp ground turmeric
1 tsp ground mixed spice
150 ml/5 fl oz Fresh Vegetable Stock (see page 16)
2 tsp sesame seeds

1 Trim, chop and prepare the French beans and set aside until required.

2 Heat the oil in a medium frying pan. Add the garlic and onion and cook over a low heat, stirring frequently, for 2 minutes. Add the tofu and cook, stirring gently occasionally, for a further 2–3 minutes, until just beginning to turn golden brown.

3 Add the French beans and broad beans. Stir in the lemon juice, turmeric, ground mixed spice and vegetable stock and bring to the boil over a medium heat.

4 Reduce the heat and simmer for about 5–7 minutes or until the beans are tender. Sprinkle with sesame seeds and serve immediately.

NUTRITION
Calories 179; Sugars 4 g; Protein 10 g; Carbohydrate 10 g; Fat 11 g; Saturates 1 g

 very easy
 10 mins
15 mins

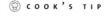 **COOK'S TIP**

Use smoked tofu instead of marinated tofu for an alternative and quite distinctive flavour.

Use large open-cap mushrooms for this recipe, both for their flavour and because they are ideal for stuffing.

Stuffed Mushrooms

1 Carefully remove the stalks from the mushrooms and chop them finely. Set aside the caps.

2 Heat the olive oil in a large, heavy-based frying pan over a medium heat. Add the chopped mushroom stalks, leek, celery, tofu, courgette and carrot and cook, stirring constantly, for 3–4 minutes.

3 Stir in the breadcrumbs, chopped basil, tomato purée and pine kernels. Season with salt and pepper to taste and mix thoroughly.

4 Divide the stuffing mixture evenly between the mushroom caps and sprinkle the grated cheese over the top. Arrange the mushrooms in a shallow ovenproof dish and pour the vegetable stock around them.

5 Cook in a preheated oven, 220°C/ 425°F/Gas Mark 7, for 20 minutes or until the mushrooms are cooked through and the cheese has melted. Remove the mushrooms from the dish and serve immediately with a salad.

SERVES 4

8 open-cap mushrooms
1 tbsp olive oil
1 small leek, chopped
1 celery stick, chopped
100 g/3½ oz firm tofu, diced
1 courgette, chopped
1 carrot, chopped
100 g/3½ oz wholemeal breadcrumbs
2 tbsp chopped fresh basil
1 tbsp tomato purée
2 tbsp pine kernels
85 g/3 oz grated Cheddar cheese
150 ml/5 fl oz Fresh Vegetable Stock
  (see page 16)
salt and pepper
salad, to serve

NUTRITION
Calories 273; Sugars 5 g; Protein 13 g;
Carbohydrate 15 g; Fat 18 g; Saturates 5 g

 very easy

 15 mins

25 mins

This imaginative and attractive recipe for artichokes stuffed with nuts, tomatoes, olives and mushrooms, has been adapted for the microwave.

Stuffed Globe Artichokes

SERVES 4

4 globe artichokes
8 tbsp water
4 tbsp lemon juice
1 onion, chopped
1 garlic clove, crushed
2 tbsp olive oil
225 g/8 oz button mushrooms, chopped
40 g/1½ oz pitted black olives, sliced
55 g/2 oz sun-dried tomatoes in oil, drained and chopped
1 tbsp chopped fresh basil
55 g/2 oz fresh white breadcrumbs
25 g/1 oz pine kernels, toasted
oil from the jar of sun-dried tomatoes, for drizzling
salt and pepper

NUTRITION
Calories 248; Sugars 8 g; Protein 5 g;
Carbohydrate 16 g; Fat 19 g; Saturates 2 g

easy

30 mins

30-35 mins

1 Cut the stalks and lower leaves off the artichokes. Snip off the leaf tips with scissors. Place 2 artichokes in a large bowl with half the water and half the lemon juice. Cover and cook in the microwave on HIGH power for 10 minutes, turning the artichokes over halfway through, until a leaf pulls away easily from the base. Leave to stand, covered, for 3 minutes before draining. Turn the artichokes upside down and leave to cool. Repeat to cook the remaining artichokes.

2 Place the onion, garlic and oil in a bowl. Cover and cook on HIGH power for 2 minutes, stirring once. Add the mushrooms, olives and sun-dried tomatoes. Cover and cook on HIGH power for 2 minutes.

3 Stir in the basil, breadcrumbs and pine kernels. Season the mixture to taste with salt and pepper.

4 Turn the artichokes the right way up and carefully pull the leaves apart. Remove the purple-tipped central leaves. Using a teaspoon, scrape out the hairy choke and discard.

5 Divide the stuffing into 4 equal portions and spoon into the centre of each artichoke. Push the leaves back around the stuffing.

6 Arrange the stuffed artichokes in a shallow dish and drizzle over a little oil from the jar of sun-dried tomatoes. Cook on HIGH power for 7–8 minutes to reheat, turning the artichokes around halfway through.

Fennel has a wonderful aniseed flavour which is ideal for grilling or barbecuing. This marinated recipe is really delicious.

Marinated Fennel

1 Cut off and reserve the fennel fronds for the garnish. Cut each of the bulbs into eight pieces and place in a shallow dish. Add the pepper and mix well.

2 To make the marinade, combine the lime juice, olive oil, garlic, mustard and thyme. Pour the marinade over the fennel and pepper and toss to coat thoroughly. Cover with clingfilm and set aside to marinate for 1 hour.

3 Thread the fennel and pepper on to wooden skewers, alternatively with the lime wedges. Cook the kebabs under a preheated medium grill, turning and basting frequently with the marinade, for about 10 minutes. Alternatively, cook on a medium hot barbecue, turning and basting frequently, for about 10 minutes.

4 Transfer the kebabs to serving plates, garnish with fennel fronds and serve immediately with a crisp salad.

SERVES 4

2 fennel bulbs
1 red pepper, halved, deseeded and cut into large dice
1 lime, cut into 8 wedges

marinade

2 tbsp lime juice
4 tbsp olive oil
2 garlic cloves, crushed
1 tsp wholegrain mustard
1 tbsp chopped fresh thyme
fennel fronds, to garnish
crisp salad, to serve

NUTRITION
Calories 117; Sugars 3 g; Protein 1 g; Carbohydrate 3 g; Fat 11 g; Saturates 2 g

 very easy
 1 hr 15 mins
1 min

very easy
1 hr 15 mins
10 mins

🍴 COOK'S TIP

Soak the skewers in cold water for 20 minutes before using to prevent them from burning during grilling. You could substitute 2 tablespoons of orange juice for the lime juice and add 1 tablespoon of honey, if you prefer.

This is so simple to prepare and looks great if you use a variety of mushrooms for shape and texture.

Garlic Mushrooms *on* Toast

SERVES 4

75 g/2¾ oz margarine
2 garlic cloves, crushed
350 g/12 oz mixed mushrooms, such as open-cap, button, oyster and shiitake, sliced
8 slices French bread
1 tbsp chopped fresh parsley
salt and pepper

1 Melt the margarine in a frying pan. Add the crushed garlic and cook, stirring constantly, for 30 seconds.

2 Add the mushrooms and cook, turning occasionally, for 5 minutes.

3 Toast the French bread slices under a preheated medium grill for 2–3 minutes, turning once. Transfer the toasts to a serving plate.

4 Toss the parsley into the mushrooms, mixing well, and season well with salt and pepper to taste.

5 Spoon the mushroom mixture over the bread and serve immediately.

NUTRITION
Calories 366; Sugars 2 g; Protein 9 g;
Carbohydrate 45 g; Fat 18 g; Saturates 4 g

 very easy

 10 mins

10 mins

Omelettes are very versatile: they go with almost anything and you can also serve them at any time of the day.

Indian-style Omelette

1 Place the chopped onion, chillies and coriander in a large mixing bowl and mix together.

2 Whisk the eggs in a separate bowl. Stir the onion mixture into the eggs. Add the salt and whisk again.

3 Heat 1 tablespoon of the oil in a large, heavy-based frying pan over a medium heat. Place a ladleful of the omelette batter in the pan. Cook the omelette, turning once and pressing down with a flat spoon to make sure that the egg is cooked right through, until the omelette is just firm and golden brown.

4 Repeat the same process with the remaining batter. Set the omelettes aside and keep them warm while you cook the remaining batter.

5 Serve the omelettes hot, garnished with the fresh basil sprigs and accompanied by toasted bread. Alternatively, simply serve the omelettes with a crisp green salad for a light lunch.

SERVES 4

1 small onion, very finely chopped
2 fresh green chillies, deseeded and chopped finely
2 tbsp finely chopped fresh coriander leaves
4 eggs
1 tsp salt
2 tbsp vegetable oil
fresh basil sprigs, to garnish
toasted bread or crisp green salad, to serve

NUTRITION
Calories 132; Sugars 1 g; Protein 7 g; Carbohydrate 2 g; Fat 11 g; Saturates 2 g

    easy

10 mins

20 mins

🏵 **COOK'S TIP**

All eggs are susceptible to bacteria. Store them in the refrigerator, with the pointed end downwards, for up to 2 weeks, and never use cracked or dirty eggs. Bring them to room temperature about 30 minutes before using.

These tasty and attractive individual tartlets are great served hot at lunchtime or cool for picnic food.

Cress *and* Cheese Tartlets

SERVES 4

100 g/3½ oz plain flour, plus extra
for dusting
pinch of salt
6 tbsp butter or margarine
2–3 tbsp cold water
2 bunches of watercress
2 garlic cloves, crushed
1 shallot, chopped
150 g/5½ oz grated Cheddar cheese
4 tbsp natural yogurt
½ tsp paprika

1 Sift the flour into a mixing bowl and add the salt. Rub 2 tablespoons of the butter or margarine into the flour until the mixture resembles breadcrumbs. Stir in enough of the cold water to make a smooth dough.

2 Roll the dough out on a lightly floured surface and use to line 4 x 10-cm/ 4-inch tartlet tins. Prick the bases with a fork and set aside to chill in the refrigerator.

3 Heat the remaining butter or margarine in a frying pan. Discard the stems from the watercress. Add the leaves to the pan with the garlic and shallot and cook for 1–2 minutes until wilted.

4 Remove the pan from the heat and stir in the grated Cheddar cheese, yogurt and paprika.

5 Spoon the mixture into the pastry cases and cook in a preheated oven, 180°C/350°F/Gas Mark 4, for 20 minutes or until the filling is just firm. Turn out the tartlets and serve immediately, if serving hot, or place on a wire rack to cool, if serving cold.

NUTRITION

Calories 410; Sugars 4 g; Protein 15 g;
Carbohydrate 24 g; Fat 29 g; Saturates 19 g

  moderate

  20 mins

  25 mins

🍲 **COOK'S TIP**

Use spinach instead of the watercress, making sure it is well drained before mixing with the remaining filling ingredients.

These are a delicious addition to any party buffet, and very simple to prepare. Serve with a sweet chilli sauce.

Sweetcorn Patties

1 Mash the drained sweetcorn lightly in a medium-sized bowl. Add the onion, curry powder, garlic, ground coriander, spring onions, flour, baking powder and egg. Stir well to combine thoroughly and season to taste with salt.

2 Heat the sunflower oil in a frying pan. Drop tablespoonfuls of the mixture carefully into the hot oil, far enough apart for them not to run into each other as they cook.

3 Cook for about 4–5 minutes, turning each patty once, until they are golden brown and firm to the touch. Take care not to turn them too soon, or they will break up in the pan.

4 Carefully remove the patties from the pan with a slice and drain them well on absorbent kitchen paper. Serve immediately while still warm garnished with extra spring onions.

SERVES 4

325 g/11½ oz canned sweetcorn kernels, drained
1 onion, chopped finely
1 tsp curry powder
1 garlic clove, crushed
1 tsp ground coriander
2 spring onions, chopped
3 tbsp plain flour
½ tsp baking powder
1 large egg
4 tbsp sunflower oil
salt
spring onions, sliced diagonally, to garnish

NUTRITION
Calories 90; Sugars 3 g; Protein 2 g;
Carbohydrate 11 g; Fat 5 g; Saturates 0.6 g

 easy

 10 mins

 10 mins

🍲 **COOK'S TIP**

To make this dish more attractive, you can serve the patties on large leaves, like the banana leaves shown in the photograph. Be sure to cut the spring onions on the diagonal, as shown, for a more elegant appearance.

This substantial version of cheese on toast – a creamy cheese sauce topped with a poached egg – makes a tasty, filling snack.

Buck Rarebit

SERVES 4

350 g/12 oz mature Cheddar
125 g/4¹/₂ oz Gouda, Gruyère or
  Emmenthal cheese
1 tsp mustard powder
1 tsp wholegrain mustard
2-4 tbsp brown ale, cider or milk
¹/₂ tsp vegetarian Worcestershire sauce
4 thick slices white or brown bread
4 eggs
salt and pepper

to garnish
tomato wedges
watercress sprigs

1 Grate the cheeses and place in a non-stick saucepan.

2 Add the mustards, seasoning, brown ale, and the vegetarian Worcestershire sauce and mix well.

3 Heat the cheese mixture gently, stirring until it has melted and is completely thick and creamy. Remove from the heat and leave to cool a little.

4 Toast the slices of bread on each side under a preheated grill then spread the rarebit mixture evenly over 1 side of each piece. Put under a moderate grill until golden brown and bubbling.

5 Meanwhile, poach the eggs. If using a poacher, grease the cups, heat the water in the pan and, when just boiling, break the eggs into the cups. Cover and simmer for 4–5 minutes until just set. Alternatively, bring about 4-cm/1¹/₂ -inches of water to the boil in a frying pan or large saucepan and for each egg quickly swirl the water with a knife and drop the egg into the 'hole' created. Cook for about 4 minutes until just set.

6 Top the rarebits with a poached egg and serve garnished with tomato wedges and watercress sprigs.

NUTRITION
Calories 478; Sugars 2 g; Protein 29 g;
Carbohydrate 14 g; Fat 34 g; Saturates 20 g

 very easy
 10 mins
 15–20 mins

🍳 **COOK'S TIP**

For a change, you can use part or all Stilton or other blue cheese; the appearance is not so attractive but the flavour is very good.

These mildly spiced croquettes are an ideal light lunch served with a crisp salad and a tahini dip.

Lentil Croquettes

1 Put the lentils in a large saucepan with the pepper, onion, garlic, garam masala, chilli powder, ground cumin, lemon juice and peanuts. Add the water and bring to the boil. Reduce the heat and simmer gently, stirring occasionally, for about 30 minutes or until all the liquid has been absorbed.

2 Remove the mixture from the heat and set aside to cool slightly. Beat in the egg and season to taste with salt and pepper. Set aside to cool completely.

3 With floured hands, form the mixture into 8 rectangles or ovals.

4 Combine the flour, turmeric and chilli powder on a small plate. Roll the croquettes in the spiced flour mixture to coat thoroughly.

5 Heat the vegetable oil in a large frying pan. Add the croquettes to the pan, cooking them in 2 batches if necessary. Fry for about 10 minutes, turning once carefully to prevent the croquettes breaking up, until they are crisp and lightly coloured on both sides.

6 Transfer the croquettes to warmed serving plates and serve them immediately with a garnish of crisp salad leaves and fresh herbs.

SERVES 4

225 g/8 oz split red lentils, washed
1 green pepper, halved, deseeded and chopped finely
1 red onion, chopped finely
2 garlic cloves, crushed
1 tsp garam masala
½ tsp chilli powder
1 tsp ground cumin
2 tsp lemon juice
2 tbsp chopped unsalted peanuts
600 ml/1 pint water
1 egg, beaten
3 tbsp plain flour
1 tsp ground turmeric
1 tsp chilli powder
4 tbsp vegetable oil
salt and pepper
salad leaves and fresh herbs, to serve

NUTRITION
Calories 409; Sugars 5 g; Protein 19 g; Carbohydrate 48 g; Fat 17 g; Saturates 2 g

   easy

40 mins

50 mins

These appetizing little cakes are packed with creamy potato and a variety of mushrooms, and make a quick and satisfying snack.

Mixed Mushroom Cakes

SERVES 4

500 g/1 lb 2 oz floury potatoes, diced
2 tbsp butter
175 g/6 oz mixed mushrooms, chopped
2 garlic cloves, crushed
1 small egg, beaten
1 tbsp chopped fresh chives, plus extra
  to garnish
flour, for dusting
oil, for frying
salt and pepper
crisp salad, to serve

1 Cook the potatoes in a pan of lightly salted boiling water for 10 minutes, or until cooked through.

2 Drain the potatoes well, mash with a potato masher or fork and set aside.

3 Meanwhile, melt the butter in a frying pan. Add the mushrooms and garlic and cook, stirring constantly, for 5 minutes. Drain well.

4 Stir the mushrooms and garlic into the potatoes, together with the beaten egg and chives.

5 Divide the mixture equally into 4 portions and shape them into round cakes. Toss the cakes in the flour until they are completely coated.

6 Heat the oil in a frying pan. Add the potato cakes and fry over a medium heat for 10 minutes until they are golden brown, turning them over carefully halfway through.

7 Garnish the cakes with the chives and serve immediately, with a crisp salad.

NUTRITION
Calories 298; Sugars 0 .8g; Protein 5 g;
Carbohydrate 22 g; Fat 22 g; Saturates 5 g

easy

20 mins

25 mins

You can use dried chickpeas for this popular snack, but the canned sort are quick and easy without sacrificing much flavour.

Bombay Bowl

1 Drain the chickpeas and place them in a bowl.

2 Place the diced potatoes in a saucepan of water and boil until cooked through. Test by inserting the tip of a knife into the potatoes – they should feel soft and tender. Drain and set the potatoes aside until required.

3 Mix together the tamarind paste and water in a small mixing bowl.

4 Add the chilli powder, sugar and salt to the tamarind paste mixture and stir well to combine. Pour the mixture over the chickpeas.

5 Add the chopped onion and the diced potatoes, and stir to mix. Season to taste with a little salt.

6 Transfer the mixture to a serving bowl and garnish with the sliced tomato, chopped chillies and coriander leaves.

SERVES 4

400 g/14 oz canned chickpeas
2 medium potatoes, diced
2 tbsp tamarind paste
6 tbsp water
1 tsp chilli powder
2 tsp sugar
1 medium onion, chopped finely
1 tsp salt

to garnish
1 tomato, sliced
2 fresh green chillies, chopped
fresh coriander leaves

NUTRITION
Calories *183*; Sugars *6 g*; Protein *9 g*;
Carbohydrate *33 g*; Fat *3 g*; Saturates *0.3 g*

     easy

15 mins

15 mins

🍪 **COOK'S TIP**

Cream-coloured and resembling a hazelnut in appearance, chickpeas have a distinctive nutty flavour and slightly crunchy texture.

This dish is extremely
versatile – it could be
made with any vegetables
that you have to hand,
and basmati rice instead
of brown.

Brown Rice Gratin

SERVES 4

100 g/3¹/₂ oz brown rice
2 tbsp butter or margarine, plus extra
    for greasing
1 red onion, chopped
2 garlic cloves, crushed
1 carrot, cut into thin batons
1 courgette, sliced
85 g/3 oz baby corn cobs, halved lengthways
2 tbsp sunflower seeds
3 tbsp chopped fresh mixed herbs
100 g/3¹/₂ oz grated mozzarella cheese
2 tbsp wholemeal breadcrumbs
salt and pepper

1 Cook the rice in a pan of lightly salted boiling water for 20 minutes until tender. Drain well.

2 Lightly grease an 850 ml/1¹/₂ pint ovenproof dish with butter.

3 Melt the butter or margarine in a frying pan. Cook the onion over a low heat, stirring constantly, for 2 minutes or until soft.

4 Add the garlic, carrot, courgette and baby corn cobs and cook, stirring constantly, for a further 5 minutes until the vegetables are softened.

5 Combine the drained rice with the sunflower seeds and mixed herbs and stir into the pan. Stir in half of the mozzarella cheese and season with salt and pepper to taste.

6 Spoon the mixture into the prepared dish and top with the breadcrumbs and remaining cheese.

7 Cook in a preheated oven, 180°C/350°F/Gas Mark 4, for about 25–30 minutes or until the cheese has begun to turn golden. Serve immediately.

NUTRITION
Calories 321; Sugars 6 g; Protein 10 g;
Carbohydrate 32 g; Fat 18 g; Saturates 9 g

easy

15 mins

1 hr

These grated potato cakes are also known as straw cakes, because they resemble a straw mat. Serve them with a tomato sauce or salad.

Cheese *and* Onion Rostis

1 Parboil the potatoes in a pan of lightly salted boiling water for 10 minutes and leave to cool. Peel the potatoes and grate with a coarse grater. Place the grated potatoes in a large mixing bowl.

2 Stir in the onion, cheese and parsley. Season well with salt and pepper. Divide the potato mixture into 4 portions of equal size and form them into cakes.

3 Heat half of the olive oil and butter in a frying pan and cook 2 of the potato cakes over a high heat for 1 minute, then reduce the heat and cook for 5 minutes, until they are golden underneath. Turn them over and cook for a further 5 minutes.

4 Repeat with the other half of the oil and the remaining butter to cook the remaining 2 cakes. Transfer to warm individual serving plates, garnish and serve immediately.

SERVES 4

900 g/2 lb potatoes
1 onion, grated
50 g/1³/₄ oz Gruyère cheese, grated
2 tbsp chopped fresh parsley
1 tbsp olive oil
2 tbsp butter
salt and pepper

to garnish
1 spring onion, shredded
1 small tomato, quartered

NUTRITION
Calories *307*; Sugars *4 g*; Protein *8 g*;
Carbohydrate *42 g*; Fat *13 g*; Saturates *6 g*

  easy
  10 mins
  40 mins

COOK'S TIP

The potato cakes should be flattened as much as possible during cooking, otherwise the outsides will be cooked before the centres are done.

A hot cheese dip made from three different cheeses can be prepared easily and with guaranteed success in the microwave.

Three-cheese Fondue

SERVES 4

1 garlic clove
300 ml/10 fl oz dry white wine
250 g/8 oz grated mild Cheddar cheese
125 g/4½ oz grated Gruyère cheese
125 g/4½ oz grated mozzarella cheese
2 tbsp cornflour
pepper

to serve
French bread
vegetables, such as courgettes, mushrooms,
   baby corn cobs and cauliflower

1 Bruise the garlic by placing the flat side of a knife on top and pressing down with the heel of your hand.

2 Rub the garlic around the inside of a large bowl. Discard the garlic.

3 Pour the wine into the bowl and heat, uncovered, in the microwave, on HIGH power for 3–4 minutes, until hot, but not boiling.

4 Gradually add the Cheddar and Gruyère cheeses, stirring well after each addition (see Cook's Tip), then add the mozzarella. Stir until all the cheese is completely melted.

5 Mix the cornflour with a little water to form a smooth paste and stir it into the cheese mixture. Season to taste with pepper.

6 Cover and cook on MEDIUM power for 6 minutes, stirring twice during cooking, until the sauce is smooth.

7 Cut the French bread into bite-sized cubes and the vegetables into batons, slices or florets. To serve, keep the fondue warm over a spirit lamp or reheat as necessary in the microwave oven. Dip in cubes of French bread and batons, slices or vegetable florets.

COOK'S TIP

Make sure you add the cheese to the wine gradually, mixing well in between each addition, to prevent the mixture from curdling.

NUTRITION
Calories 565; Sugars 1 g; Protein 29 g;
Carbohydrate 15 g; Fat 38 g; Saturates 24 g

 very easy
 15 mins
10 mins

Golden potato slices coated in breadcrumbs and cheese are a delicious light meal at any time of day.

Cheese *and* Potato Slices

1 Cook the potatoes in a saucepan of boiling water for about 10–15 minutes, or until the potatoes are just tender. Drain thoroughly.

2 Mix the breadcrumbs, cheese and chilli powder together in a bowl, then transfer to a shallow dish. Pour the eggs into a separate shallow dish.

3 Dip the potato slices first in egg and then roll them in the breadcrumbs to coat completely.

4 Heat the oil in a large saucepan or deep-fryer to 180°C/350°F or until a cube of bread browns in 30 seconds. Cook the cheese and potato slices, in several batches, for 4–5 minutes or until they turn a golden brown colour.

5 Remove the cheese and potato slices from the oil with a slotted spoon and drain thoroughly on kitchen paper. Keep the cheese and potato slices warm while you cook the remaining batches.

6 Transfer the cheese and potato slices to warm individual serving plates. Dust lightly with chilli powder, if using, and serve immediately.

SERVES 4

900 g/2 lb waxy potatoes, unpeeled and sliced thickly
70 g/2½ oz fresh white breadcrumbs
40 g/1½ oz Parmesan cheese, freshly grated
1½ tsp chilli powder
2 eggs, beaten
oil, for deep frying
chilli powder, for dusting (optional)

NUTRITION
Calories 560; Sugars 3 g; Protein 19 g;
Carbohydrate 55 g; Fat 31 g; Saturates 7 g

COOK'S TIP

The potato slices may be coated in the cheese and breadcrumb mixture in advance and then stored in the refrigerator until ready to use.

 easy

 10 mins

40 mins

Pasta, Grains *and* Pulses

Pasta is one of the most popular and versatile ingredients available, and it is both nourishing and satisfying. Fresh or dried pasta is made in a variety of flavours and colours, shapes and sizes, all of which work well with a number of vegetarian sauces. Pasta combines well with vegetables, herbs, nuts and cheeses to provide scores of interesting and tasty meals. Noodles are also quick to cook and provide good basic food that can be dressed up in all kinds of different ways. Often flavoured with oriental ingredients, the noodle recipes in this chapter are sure to liven up a vegetarian diet, as are the tantalizing rice and pulses meals included here.

This pasta dish is baked in a pudding basin and cut into slices for serving. It looks and tastes terrific and is perfect when you want to impress.

Tomato *and* Pasta Bake

SERVES 4

100 g/3½ oz pasta shapes, such as
  penne or casareccia
1 tbsp olive oil
1 leek, chopped
3 garlic cloves, crushed
1 green pepper, halved, deseeded
  and chopped
400 g/14 oz canned chopped tomatoes
2 tbsp chopped, pitted black olives
2 eggs, beaten
1 tbsp chopped fresh basil

tomato sauce
1 tbsp olive oil
1 onion, chopped
225 g/8 oz canned chopped tomatoes
1 tsp caster sugar
2 tbsp tomato purée
150 ml/¼ fl oz Fresh Vegetable Stock
  (see page 16)
salt and pepper

NUTRITION
Calories *179*; Sugars *6 g*; Protein *8 g*;
Carbohydrate *16 g*; Fat *10 g*; Saturates *3 g*

moderate

10 mins

1 hr 5 mins

1 Cook the pasta in a saucepan of boiling salted water for 8 minutes, then drain thoroughly.

2 Meanwhile, heat the olive oil in a saucepan and sauté the leek and garlic for 2 minutes, stirring constantly. Add the pepper, tomatoes and olives to the pan and cook for a further 5 minutes.

3 Remove the pan from the heat and stir in the pasta, beaten eggs and basil. Season well, and spoon into a lightly greased 1 litre/2 pint ovenproof pudding basin.

4 Place the pudding basin in a roasting tin and half-fill the tin with boiling water. Cover the pudding and cook in a preheated oven, 180°C/350°F/Gas Mark 6, for 40 minutes until set.

5 To make the sauce, heat the olive oil in a pan and sauté the onion for 2 minutes. Add the remaining ingredients to the pan and cook for a further 10 minutes. Put the sauce in a food processor or blender and blend until smooth. Return to a clean saucepan and heat through again until hot.

6 Turn the pasta out of the pudding basin on to a warm plate. Slice and serve with the tomato sauce.

This dish is made with prepared cannelloni tubes, but may also be made by rolling ready-bought lasagne sheets.

Vegetable Cannelloni

1 Heat the oil in a frying pan. Add the aubergine and cook over a moderate heat, stirring frequently, for 2–3 minutes.

2 Add the spinach, garlic, cumin and mushrooms and reduce the heat. Season to taste with salt and pepper and cook, stirring constantly, for 2–3 minutes. Spoon the mixture into the cannelloni tubes and place in an ovenproof dish in a single layer.

3 To make the sauce, heat the olive oil in a pan and cook the onion and garlic for 1 minute. Add the tomatoes, sugar and basil and bring to the boil. Reduce the heat and simmer gently for about 5 minutes. Spoon the sauce over the cannelloni tubes.

4 Arrange the sliced mozzarella on top of the sauce and cook in a preheated oven, 190°C/375°F/Gas Mark 5, for about 30 minutes or until the cheese is bubbling and golden brown. Serve immediately.

SERVES 4

125 ml/4 fl oz olive oil
1 aubergine
225 g/8 oz spinach
2 garlic cloves, crushed
1 tsp ground cumin
85 g/3 oz mushrooms, chopped
12 cannelloni tubes
salt and pepper

tomato sauce
1 tbsp olive oil
1 onion, chopped
2 garlic cloves, crushed
800 g/1lb 12 oz canned chopped tomatoes
1 tsp caster sugar
2 tbsp chopped fresh basil
55 g/2 oz sliced mozzarella

NUTRITION
Calories 594; Sugars 12 g; Protein 13 g;
Carbohydrate 52 g; Fat 38 g; Saturates 7 g

✪✪✪   moderate
        30 mins
        45 mins

This colourful and tasty lasagne contains layers of vegetables in tomato sauce, all topped with a rich cheese sauce.

Vegetable Lasagne

SERVES 4

1 aubergine, sliced
3 tbsp olive oil
2 garlic cloves, crushed
1 red onion, halved and sliced
3 mixed peppers, halved, deseeded and diced
225 g/8 oz mixed mushrooms, sliced
2 celery sticks, sliced
1 courgette, diced
½ tsp each chilli powder and ground cumin
2 tomatoes, chopped
300 ml/10fl oz passata
2 tbsp chopped fresh basil
8 pre-cooked lasagne verde sheets
salt and pepper

cheese sauce
2 tbsp butter or margarine
1 tbsp flour
150 ml/5 fl oz Fresh Vegetable Stock
300 ml/10 fl oz milk
75 g/2¾ oz grated Cheddar cheese
1 tsp Dijon mustard
1 tbsp chopped fresh basil
1 egg, beaten

NUTRITION

Calories 544; Sugars 18 g; Protein 20 g;
Carbohydrate 61 g; Fat 26 g; Saturates 12 g

✪✪✪   moderate

🕐   35 mins

🕐   55 mins

1   Place the aubergine slices in a colander, sprinkle them with salt and leave for 20 minutes. Rinse under cold water, drain and reserve.

2   Heat the oil in a saucepan and sauté the garlic and onion for 1–2 minutes. Add the peppers, mushrooms, celery and courgette and cook, stirring constantly, for 3–4 minutes.

3   Stir in the spices and cook for 1 minute. Mix in the chopped tomatoes, passata and basil and season to taste with salt and pepper.

4   For the sauce, melt the butter in a pan, stir in the flour and cook for 1 minute. Remove from the heat, stir in the stock and milk, return to the heat and add half the cheese and the mustard. Boil, stirring, until thickened. Stir in the basil. Remove from the heat and stir in the egg.

5   Place half the lasagne sheets in an ovenproof dish. Top with half the vegetable mixture, then half the aubergines. Repeat the layers and spoon the cheese sauce over the top.

6   Sprinkle the lasagne with the remaining cheese and cook in a preheated oven, 180°C/350°F/ Gas 4, for 40 minutes, until the top is golden brown.

Use any pasta shapes that you have for this recipe – fusilli were used here. Multi-coloured pasta is visually the most attractive to use.

Spinach *and* Nut Pasta

1 Bring a large pan of lightly salted water to the boil. Add the pasta, bring back to the boil and cook for 8–10 minutes until tender, but still firm to the bite. Drain well.

2 Meanwhile, heat the oil in a large saucepan. Add the garlic and onion and cook over a low heat, stirring occasionally, for 1 minute.

3 Add the sliced mushrooms to the pan and cook over a medium heat, stirring occasionally, for 2 minutes.

4 Lower the heat, add the spinach and cook, stirring occasionally, for a further 4–5 minutes or until the spinach has just wilted.

5 Stir in the pine kernels and wine, season to taste with salt and pepper and cook for 1 minute.

6 Transfer the pasta to a warm serving bowl and toss the sauce into it, mixing well. Garnish with shavings of Parmesan cheese and serve immediately.

SERVES 4

225 g/8 oz dried pasta shapes
125 ml/4 fl oz olive oil
2 garlic cloves, crushed
1 onion, quartered and sliced
3 large flat mushrooms, sliced
225 g/8 oz spinach
2 tbsp pine kernels
5 tbsp dry white wine
salt and pepper
Parmesan shavings, to garnish

NUTRITION
Calories 603; Sugars 5 g; Protein 12 g;
Carbohydrate 46 g; Fat 41 g; Saturates 6 g

 very easy

 5 mins

15 mins

COOK'S TIP

Grate a little nutmeg over the dish for extra flavour, as this spice has a particular affinity with spinach.

This dish is considered the Thai national dish, as it is made and eaten everywhere – a one-dish, fast food for eating on the move.

Thai-style Stir-fried Noodles

SERVES 4

225 g/8 oz dried rice noodles
2 red chillies, deseeded and chopped finely
2 shallots, chopped finely
2 tbsp sugar
2 tbsp tamarind water
1 tbsp lime juice
2 tbsp light soy sauce
1 tbsp sunflower oil
1 tsp sesame oil
175 g/6 oz diced smoked tofu
pepper
2 tbsp chopped roasted peanuts, to garnish

1 Cook the rice noodles as directed on the pack, or soak them in boiling water for 5 minutes.

2 Grind together the chillies, shallots, sugar, tamarind water, lime juice, light soy sauce and pepper to taste.

3 Heat the sunflower and sesame oils together in a preheated wok or large, heavy frying pan over a high heat. Add the tofu and stir-fry for 1 minute.

4 Add the chilli mixture, bring to the boil, and continue to cook, stirring constantly, for about 2 minutes, until the sauce has thickened.

5 Drain the rice noodles and add them to the chilli mixture. Use 2 spoons to lift and stir the noodles until they are no longer steaming.

6 Serve the hot noodles immediately, garnished with the chopped peanuts.

NUTRITION
Calories 407; Sugars 11 g; Protein 14 g;
Carbohydrate 56 g; Fat 16 g; Saturates 3 g

very easy

15 mins

8 mins

 **COOK'S TIP**

This is a quick one-dish meal that is very useful if you are catering for a single vegetarian in the family.

This quick dish is an ideal lunchtime meal, packed with mixed mushrooms in a sweet sauce.

Stir-Fried Japanese Noodles

1 Place the Japanese egg noodles in a large bowl. Pour over enough boiling water to cover and leave them to soak for 10 minutes.

2 Heat the sunflower oil in a large preheated wok.

3 Add the red onion and garlic to the wok and stir-fry for 2–3 minutes, or until softened.

4 Add the mushrooms to the wok and stir-fry for about 5 minutes, or until the mushrooms have softened.

5 Drain the egg noodles thoroughly and set aside.

6 Add the pak choi (or Chinese leaves), noodles, sweet sherry and oyster sauce to the wok. Toss all of the ingredients together and stir-fry for 2–3 minutes or until the liquid is just beginning to bubble.

7 Transfer the mushroom noodles to warm serving bowls and scatter with sliced spring onions and toasted sesame seeds. Serve immediately.

SERVES 4

250 g/9 oz Japanese egg noodles
2 tbsp sunflower oil
1 red onion, sliced
1 garlic clove, crushed
450 g/1 lb mixed mushrooms (shiitake, oyster, brown cap)
350 g/12 oz pak choi (or Chinese leaves)
2 tbsp sweet sherry
6 tbsp oyster sauce
4 spring onions, sliced
1 tbsp toasted sesame seeds

NUTRITION
Calories 379; Sugars 8 g; Protein 12 g; Carbohydrate 53 g; Fat 13 g; Saturates 3 g

easy

15 mins

20-25 mins

🍲 COOK'S TIP

The variety of mushrooms in supermarkets has greatly improved and a good mixture should be easily obtainable. If not, use the more common button and flat mushrooms.

In this simple recipe, cooked rice is fried with vegetables and cashew nuts. It can either be eaten on its own or served as an accompaniment.

Special Fried Rice

SERVES 4

175 g/6 oz long grain rice
55 g/2 oz cashew nuts
2 tbsp vegetable oil
1 carrot, halved lengthways and sliced
½ cucumber, halved, deseeded and sliced
1 yellow pepper, halved, deseeded and sliced
2 spring onions, chopped
1 garlic clove, crushed
125 g/4½ oz frozen peas, thawed
1 tbsp soy sauce
1 tsp salt
fresh coriander leaves, to garnish

1 Bring a large saucepan of water to the boil. Add the rice to the pan and simmer for 15 minutes. Tip the rice into a sieve and rinse; drain thoroughly.

2 Heat a wok or large, heavy-based frying pan, add the cashew nuts and dry-fry until lightly browned. Remove and set aside.

3 Heat the oil in a wok or large frying pan. Add the vegetables and the garlic. Stir-fry for 3 minutes. Add the rice, peas, soy sauce and salt. Continue to stir-fry until the vegetables are well mixed and thoroughly heated.

4 Stir in the reserved cashew nuts. Transfer to a warmed serving dish, garnish with the coriander leaves and serve immediately.

NUTRITION

Calories 355; Sugars 6 g; Protein 9 g;
Carbohydrate 48 g; Fat 15 g; Saturates 3 g

easy

10 mins

30 mins

🐧 COOK'S TIP

You can replace any of the vegetables in this recipe with others suitable for a stir-fry, and using leftover rice makes this a perfect last-minute dish.

Egg noodles are cooked
and then fried with
a colourful variety
of vegetables to make
this well-known,
and ever-popular dish.

Chow Mein

1 Cook the egg noodles according to the packet instructions. Drain and rinse under cold running water until cool. Set aside.

2 Heat 3 tablespoons of the vegetable oil in a preheated wok or frying pan. Add the onion and carrots and stir-fry for 1 minute, then add the mushrooms, mangetout and cucumber and stir-fry for a further 1 minute.

3 Stir in the remaining vegetable oil and add the drained noodles, together with the spinach and beansprouts.

4 Blend together all the remaining ingredients and pour the mixture over the noodles and vegetables.

5 Stir-fry until the noodle mixture is thoroughly heated through, transfer to a warm serving dish and serve.

SERVES 4

500 g/1 lb 2 oz egg noodles
4 tbsp vegetable oil
1 onion, thinly sliced
2 carrots, cut into thin sticks
125 g/4¹/₂ oz button mushrooms, quartered
125 g/4¹/₂ oz mangetout
¹/₂ cucumber, cut into sticks
125 g/4¹/₂ oz spinach, shredded
125 g/4¹/₂ oz beansprouts
2 tbsp dark soy sauce
1 tbsp sherry
1 tsp salt
1 tsp sugar
1 tsp cornflour
1 tsp sesame oil

NUTRITION
Calories *669*; Sugars *9 g*; Protein *19 g*;
Carbohydrate *100 g*; Fat *23 g*; Saturates *4 g*

 very easy

 15 mins

10 mins

🅒 COOK'S TIP

For a spicy hot chow mein, add 1 tablespoon chilli sauce or substitute chilli oil for the sesame oil.

Young spinach and fresh herbs are the basis of this colourful, refreshing and summery risotto.

Risotto Verde

SERVES 4

1.7 litres/3 pints Fresh Vegetable Stock (see page 16)
2 tbsp olive oil
2 garlic cloves, crushed
2 leeks, shredded
225 g/8 oz arborio rice
300 ml/10 fl oz dry white wine
4 tbsp chopped mixed fresh herbs
225 g/8 oz young spinach
3 tbsp low-fat natural yogurt
salt and pepper
shredded leek, to garnish

1 Pour the stock into a large saucepan and bring it to the boil, then reduce the heat to a simmer.

2 Meanwhile, heat the oil in a separate saucepan and cook the garlic and leeks, stirring occasionally, for 2–3 minutes, until softened, but not browned.

3 Stir in the rice and cook, stirring constantly, until translucent and well coated with oil.

4 Pour in half of the wine and a little of the hot stock; it will bubble and steam rapidly. Cook over a gentle heat, stirring, until all of the liquid has been absorbed.

5 Add the remaining stock and wine and cook over a low heat for 25 minutes or until the rice is creamy, stirring all the time.

6 Stir in the mixed herbs and the young spinach, season to taste with salt and pepper and cook for a further 2 minutes. Stir in the yogurt.

7 Garnish with the shredded leek and serve the risotto immediately.

NUTRITION

Calories 374; Sugars 5 g; Protein 10 g;
Carbohydrate 55 g; Fat 9 g; Saturates 2 g

moderate

5 mins

45 mins

🍽 **COOK'S TIP**

Do not hurry the process of cooking the risotto as the rice must absorb the liquid slowly in order for it to reach the correct consistency.

An aubergine is halved and filled with a risotto mixture, topped with cheese and baked to make a snack or quick meal for two.

Risotto *in* Shells

1 Cook the rice in boiling salted water for about 15 minutes, until just tender. Drain, rinse and drain again.

2 Bring a large saucepan of water to the boil. Cut the stem off the aubergine and cut the aubergine in half lengthways. Cut out the flesh from the centre carefully, leaving about a 1.5-cm/½-inch shell. Blanch the shells in the boiling water for 3–4 minutes. Drain thoroughly. Chop the aubergine flesh finely.

3 Heat the olive oil in a saucepan or frying pan. Add the onion and garlic and fry over a low heat until beginning to soften, then add the pepper and aubergine flesh and continue cooking for 2–3 minutes. Add the water to the pan and cook for a further 2–3 minutes.

4 Remove the pan from the heat, stir the raisins, chopped cashew nuts, dried oregano and cooked rice into the aubergine mixture, and season to taste with salt and pepper.

5 Place the aubergine shells in an ovenproof dish and spoon in the rice mixture, piling it up well. Cover and cook in a preheated oven, 190°C/375°F/Gas Mark 5, for 20 minutes.

6 Remove the cover and sprinkle the grated Cheddar or Parmesan cheese over the rice, covering it evenly. Place the dish under a preheated moderate grill and cook for 3–4 minutes, until golden brown and bubbling. Serve hot garnished with oregano or parsley.

SERVES 2

55 g/2 oz mixed long grain and wild rice
1 aubergine, about 350 g/12 oz
1 tbsp olive oil
1 small onion, chopped finely
1 garlic clove, crushed
½ small red pepper, halved, deseeded and chopped
2 tbsp water
25 g/1 oz raisins
25 g/1 oz cashew nuts, chopped roughly
½ tsp dried oregano
40 g/1½ oz grated mature Cheddar or Parmesan cheese
salt and pepper
fresh oregano or parsley, to garnish

NUTRITION
Calories *444*; Sugars *20 g*; Protein *13 g*; Carbohydrate *50 g*; Fat *23 g*; Saturates *8 g*

✪✪✪ moderate
 20 mins
 55 mins

Cajun spices add a flavour of the American Deep South to this colourful rice and red kidney bean salad.

Deep South Rice *and* Beans

SERVES 4

175 g/6 oz long grain rice
4 tbsp olive oil
1 small green pepper, halved, deseeded and chopped
1 small red pepper, halved, deseeded and chopped
1 onion, chopped finely
1 small fresh red or green chilli, deseeded and chopped finely
2 tomatoes, chopped
125 g/4½ oz canned red kidney beans, rinsed and drained
1 tbsp chopped fresh basil
2 tsp chopped fresh thyme
1 tsp Cajun spice
salt and pepper
fresh basil leaves, to garnish

1 Cook the rice in plenty of boiling, lightly salted water for about 12 minutes, until it is just tender. Rinse under cold water, drain well and set aside.

2 Meanwhile, heat the olive oil in a frying pan, add the green and red peppers and the onion and fry gently for about 5 minutes, until softened.

3 Add the chilli and tomatoes, and cook for a further 2 minutes.

4 Add the vegetable mixture and the drained red kidney beans to the rice. Stir well to combine thoroughly.

5 Stir the chopped fresh herbs and the Cajun spice into the rice mixture.

6 Season the salad to taste with salt and pepper, and serve, garnished with fresh basil leaves.

NUTRITION
Calories *336*; Sugars *8 g*; Protein *7 g*; Carbohydrate *51 g*; Fat *13 g*; Saturates *2 g*

very easy

10 mins

20 mins

The whole spices are not meant to be eaten and may be removed before serving. Omit the broccoli and mushrooms for a plain, spiced pilau.

Spiced Basmati Pilau

1 Place the rice in a sieve and wash well under cold running water. Drain. Trim off most of the broccoli stalk and cut into small florets, then quarter the stalk lengthways and cut diagonally into 1-cm/½-inch pieces.

2 Heat the oil in a large saucepan. Add the onions and broccoli stalks and cook over a low heat, stirring frequently, for 3 minutes. Add the mushrooms, rice, garlic and spices and cook for 1 minute, stirring, until the rice is coated in oil.

3 Add the boiling stock and season to taste with salt and pepper. Stir in the broccoli florets and return the mixture to the boil. Cover, reduce the heat and cook over a low heat for 15 minutes without uncovering the pan.

4 Remove the pan from the heat and leave the pilau to stand for 5 minutes without uncovering. Remove the whole spices, add the raisins and pistachios and gently fork through to fluff up the grains. Serve the pilau hot.

SERVES 4

500 g/1 lb 2 oz basmati rice
175 g/6 oz broccoli, trimmed
6 tbsp vegetable oil
2 large onions, chopped
225 g/8 oz sliced mushrooms
2 garlic cloves, crushed
6 cardamom pods, split
6 whole cloves
8 black peppercorns
1 cinnamon stick or piece of cassia bark
1 tsp ground turmeric
1.2 litres/2 pints boiling Fresh Vegetable Stock (see page 16) or water
salt and pepper
55 g/2 oz seedless raisins
55 g/2 oz unsalted pistachios, chopped

NUTRITION
Calories 450; Sugars 3 g; Protein 9 g;
Carbohydrate 76 g; Fat 15 g; Saturates 2 g

easy

20 mins

20 mins

(🍴) **COOK'S TIP**

For added richness, you could stir a tablespoon of vegetable ghee through the rice mixture just before serving. A little diced red pepper and a few cooked peas forked through in step 4 add a colourful touch.

Every Thai meal has, as its centrepiece, a big bowl of steaming, fluffy Thai jasmine rice, to which salt should not be added.

Thai Jasmine Rice

SERVES 4

open pan method
225 g/8 oz Thai jasmine rice
1 litre/1¾ pints water

absorption method
225 g/8 oz Thai jasmine rice
450 ml/16 fl oz water

1 For the open pan method, rinse the rice in a sieve under cold running water and leave to drain.

2 Bring the water to the boil. Add the rice, stir once and return to a medium boil. Cook, uncovered, for 8–10 minutes, until tender.

3 Drain thoroughly and fork through lightly before serving.

1 For the absorption method, rinse the rice under cold running water.

2 Put the rice and water into a saucepan and bring to the boil. Stir once and then cover the pan tightly. Lower the heat as much as possible. Cook for 10 minutes, and leave to rest for a further 5 minutes.

3 Fork through lightly and serve the rice immediately.

NUTRITION
Calories 239; Sugars 0 g; Protein 5 g;
Carbohydrate 54 g; Fat 2 g; Saturates 0.6 g

 very easy

 5 mins

10 mins

 **COOK'S TIP**

Thai jasmine rice can be frozen. Freeze in a plastic sealed container. Frozen rice is ideal for stir-fry dishes, as the process seems to separate the grains.

Couscous is a semolina grain which is very quick and easy to cook, and it makes a pleasant change from rice or pasta.

Vegetable Couscous

1 Heat the oil in a large saucepan and fry the onion, carrot and turnip for 3–4 minutes. Add the stock, bring to the boil, cover and simmer for 20 minutes.

2 Meanwhile, put the couscous in a bowl and moisten with a little boiling water, stirring, until the grains have swollen and separated.

3 Add the tomatoes, courgettes, pepper and French beans to the saucepan.

4 Stir the lemon rind into the couscous, add the turmeric, if using, and mix thoroughly. Put the couscous in a steamer and position it over the saucepan of vegetables. Simmer the vegetables, steaming the couscous at the same time for 8–10 minutes.

5 Pile the couscous onto warmed serving plates. Ladle the vegetables over the top, together with some of their cooking liquid.

6 Scatter the vegetable couscous with the chopped coriander and serve at once, garnished with the flat-leaf parsley sprigs.

SERVES 4

2 tbsp vegetable oil
1 large onion, chopped coarsely
1 carrot, chopped
1 turnip, chopped
600 ml/1 pint Fresh Vegetable Stock
   (see page 16)
175 g/6 oz couscous
2 tomatoes, peeled and quartered
2 courgettes, chopped
1 red pepper, halved, deseeded and chopped
125 g/4½ oz French beans, chopped
grated rind of 1 lemon
pinch of ground turmeric (optional)
1 tbsp finely chopped fresh coriander
   or parsley
salt and pepper
fresh flat-leaf parsley sprigs, to garnish

NUTRITION
Calories *280*; Sugars *13 g*; Protein *10 g*;
Carbohydrate *47 g*; Fat *7 g*; Saturates *1 g*

✪✪✪   moderate
   20 mins
   40 mins

Bulgur wheat is very easy to use and, as well as being full of nutrients, it is a delicious alternative to rice, having a distinctive nutty flavour.

Bulgur Pilau

SERVES 4

6 tbsp butter or margarine
1 red onion, halved and sliced
2 garlic cloves, crushed
350 g/12 oz bulgur wheat
175 g/6 oz tomatoes, deseeded and chopped
55 g/2 oz baby corn cobs
85 g/3 oz small broccoli florets
850 ml/1½ pints Fresh Vegetable Stock
  (see page 16)
2 tbsp clear honey
55 g/2 oz sultanas
55 g/2 oz pine kernels
½ tsp ground cinnamon
½ tsp ground cumin
salt and pepper
sliced spring onions, to garnish

1 Melt the butter or margarine in a large flameproof casserole over a medium heat. Add the onion and garlic and cook, stirring occasionally, for 2–3 minutes until softened, but not browned.

2 Add the bulgur wheat, tomatoes, corn cobs, broccoli florets and vegetable stock and bring to the boil. Reduce the heat, cover and simmer gently, stirring occasionally, for 15–20 minutes.

3 Stir in the honey, sultanas, pine kernels, ground cinnamon and cumin and season with salt and pepper to taste, mixing well. Remove the casserole from the heat, and set aside, covered, for 10 minutes.

4 Spoon the bulgur pilau into a warmed serving dish. Garnish with thinly sliced spring onions and serve the pilau immediately.

NUTRITION

Calories 637; Sugars 25 g; Protein 16 g;
Carbohydrate 90 g; Fat 26 g; Saturates 11 g

easy
15 mins
35–40 mins

🍲 COOK'S TIP

The dish is left to stand for 10 minutes so that the bulgur can finish cooking and the flavours of the ingredients will mingle.

Plain boiled rice is eaten by most people in India every day, but for entertaining, a more interesting rice dish, such as this, is served.

Pilau Rice

1 Rinse the rice twice under running water and set aside until required.

2 Heat the ghee in a saucepan. Add the cardamoms, cloves and peppercorns to the pan and fry, stirring constantly, for about 1 minute.

3 Add the rice and stir-fry over a medium heat for a further 2 minutes.

4 Add the salt, saffron and water to the rice mixture and reduce the heat. Cover the pan and simmer over a low heat until the water has been totally absorbed.

5 Transfer the pilau rice to a serving dish and serve hot.

SERVES 4

200 g/7 oz basmati rice
2 tbsp vegetable ghee
3 green cardamoms
2 whole cloves
3 peppercorns
½ tsp salt
¼ tsp saffron
400 ml/14 fl oz water

NUTRITION
Calories 265; Sugars 0 g; Protein 4 g;
Carbohydrate 43 g; Fat 10 g; Saturates 6 g

✪✪✪   moderate
🕙   15 mins
🕓   20 mins

 COOK'S TIP

The most expensive of all spices, saffron strands are the stamens of a type of crocus. They give dishes a rich, golden colour, as well as adding a distinctive, slightly bitter taste. Saffron is sold as a powder or in strands.

Rice cooked with tomatoes and onions will add colour to your table, especially when garnished with green chillies and fresh coriander.

Tomato Rice

SERVES 4

150 ml/5 fl oz vegetable oil
2 medium onions, sliced
1 tsp onion seeds
1 tsp finely chopped fresh root ginger
1 tsp crushed garlic
½ tsp ground turmeric
1 tsp chilli powder
1½ tsp salt
400 g/14 oz canned tomatoes
500 g/1 lb 2 oz basmati rice
600 ml/1 pint water

to garnish
3 fresh green chillies, chopped finely
fresh coriander leaves, chopped
3 hard-boiled eggs

1 Heat the oil in a heavy-based pan. Add the onions and fry over a moderate heat, stirring frequently, for 5 minutes until golden brown.

2 Add the onion seeds, ginger, garlic, turmeric, chilli powder and salt, stirring to combine.

3 Reduce the heat, add the tomatoes and stir-fry for 10 minutes, breaking the tomatoes up.

4 Add the rice to the tomato mixture, stirring gently to coat the rice completely. Stir in the water. Cover the pan and cook over a low heat until the water has been absorbed and the rice is tender, but still has some bite.

5 Transfer the tomato rice to a warmed serving dish. Garnish with the chopped finely green chillies, coriander leaves and hard-boiled eggs. Serve the tomato rice immediately.

NUTRITION
Calories *866*; Sugars *7 g*; Protein *15 g*;
Carbohydrate *106 g*; Fat *46 g*; Saturates *6 g*

easy

10 mins

35 mins

🍲 **COOK'S TIP**

Onion seeds are always used whole in Indian cooking, often being added to pickles and sprinkled over the top of naan breads. They don't have anything to do with the vegetable, but look similar to the plant's seed, hence the name.

Fragrant basmati rice is cooked with porcini mushrooms, spinach and pistachio nuts in this easy microwave recipe.

Spinach *and* Nut Pilau

1 Place the porcini mushrooms in a small bowl. Pour over the hot water and leave to soak for 30 minutes.

2 Place the onion, garlic, ginger, chilli and oil in a large bowl. Cover and cook in the microwave on HIGH power for 2 minutes. Rinse the rice, then stir it into the bowl, together with the carrot. Cover and cook on HIGH power for 1 minute.

3 Strain and coarsely chop the mushrooms. Add the mushroom soaking liquid to the stock to make 425 ml/15 fl oz. Pour onto the rice.

4 Stir in the mushrooms, cinnamon, cloves, saffron and ½ teaspoon salt. Cover and cook on HIGH power for 10 minutes, stirring once. Leave the mixture to stand, covered, for 10 minutes.

5 Place the spinach in a large bowl. Cover and cook on HIGH power for 3½ minutes, stirring once. Drain well and chop the spinach coarsely.

6 Stir the spinach, pistachio nuts and chopped coriander into the rice.

7 Season to taste with salt and pepper and garnish with coriander leaves. Serve immediately.

SERVES 4

10 g/¼ oz dried porcini mushrooms
300 ml/10 fl oz hot water
1 onion, chopped
1 garlic clove, crushed
1 tsp grated fresh root ginger
½ fresh green chilli, deseeded and chopped
2 tbsp oil
225 g/8 oz basmati rice
1 large carrot, grated
175 ml/6 fl oz Fresh Vegetable Stock
  (see page 16)
½ tsp ground cinnamon
4 whole cloves
½ tsp saffron strands
225 g/8 oz fresh spinach, long
  stalks removed
55 g/2 oz pistachio nuts
1 tbsp chopped fresh coriander
salt and pepper
fresh coriander leaves, to garnish

NUTRITION

Calories *403*; Sugars *7 g*; Protein *10 g*;
Carbohydrate *62 g*; Fat *15 g*; Saturates *2 g*

 very easy

 55 mins

15–20 mins

The traditional breakfast plate of kedgeree reputedly has its roots in this Indian flavoured rice dish, adopted by British colonists.

Kitchouri

SERVES 4

2 tbsp vegetable ghee or butter
1 red onion, chopped finely
1 garlic clove, crushed
½ celery stick, chopped finely
1 tsp turmeric
½ tsp garam masala
1 green chilli, deseeded and chopped finely
½ tsp cumin seeds
1 tbsp chopped fresh coriander
125 g/4½ oz basmati rice, rinsed
    under cold water
125 g/4½ oz green lentils
300 ml/10 fl oz vegetable juice
600 ml/1 Fresh Vegetable Stock (see page 16)

1 Heat the ghee or butter in a large heavy-based saucepan. Add the onion, garlic and celery to the pan and cook for about 5 minutes, until soft.

2 Add the turmeric, garam masala, chopped green chilli, cumin seeds and coriander. Cook over a moderate heat, stirring constantly, for about 1 minute, until fragrant.

3 Add the rice and lentils and cook for 1 minute, until the rice is translucent.

4 Pour the vegetable juice and stock into the saucepan and bring to the boil over a medium heat. Cover the pan and simmer over a low heat, stirring occasionally, for about 20 minutes, or until the lentils are cooked (they should be tender when pressed between two fingers).

5 Transfer the kitchouri to a warmed serving dish and serve piping hot.

NUTRITION

Calories 318; Sugars 5 g; Protein 12 g;
Carbohydrate 48 g; Fat 10 g; Saturates 6 g

easy
10 mins
30 mins

🖰 COOK'S TIP

This is a versatile dish and can be served as a great-tasting and satisfying one-pot meal. It can also be served as a winter dish with tomatoes and yogurt.

Biryani originated in the north of India and was a dish reserved for festivals. The vegetables are marinated in a yogurt-based marinade.

Vegetable Biryani

1 Cook the potato, carrots and okra in a pan of boiling salted water for 7–8 minutes. Drain well and place in a large bowl. Mix with the celery, mushrooms and aubergine.

2 Mix the natural yogurt, ginger, grated onions, garlic, turmeric and curry powder and spoon over the vegetables. Set aside in a cool place to marinate for at least 2 hours.

3 Heat the butter in a heavy-based frying pan. Add the sliced onions and cook over a medium heat for 5–6 minutes, until golden brown. Remove a few onions from the pan and reserve to garnish the finished dish.

4 Cook the rice in a large saucepan of boiling water for 7 minutes. Drain thoroughly and set aside.

5 Add the marinated vegetables to the onions and cook for 10 minutes.

6 Put half of the rice in a 2 litre/3½ pint casserole dish. Spoon the vegetable mixture on top and cover with the remaining rice.

7 Cover the dish and cook the biryani in a preheated oven, 190°C/375°F/ Gas Mark 5, for 20–25 minutes, or until the rice is tender.

8 Spoon the biryani onto a serving plate, garnish with the reserved onions and coriander and serve.

SERVES 4

300 g/10½ oz potato, cubed
100 g/3½ oz baby carrots
50 g/1¾ oz okra, thickly sliced
2 celery sticks, sliced
75 g/2¾ oz baby button mushrooms
1 aubergine, halved and sliced
300 ml/10 fl oz natural yogurt
1 tbsp grated fresh root ginger
2 large onions, grated
4 garlic cloves, crushed
1 tsp turmeric
1 tbsp curry powder
2 tbsp butter
2 onions, sliced
225 g/8 oz basmati rice
chopped fresh coriander, to garnish

NUTRITION
Calories *449*; Sugars *18 g*; Protein *12 g*;
Carbohydrate *79 g*; Fat *12 g*; Saturates *6 g*

moderate

2 hrs 15 mins

1 hr

Aloo Chat is one of a variety of Indian foods served at any time of the day. The chickpeas need to be soaked overnight.

Aloo Chat

SERVES 4

125 g/4¹/₂ oz chickpeas, soaked overnight in cold water and drained
1 dried red chilli
500 g/1 lb 2 oz waxy potatoes, boiled in their skins and peeled
1 tsp cumin seeds
2 tsp salt
1 tsp black peppercorns
¹/₂ tsp dried mint
¹/₂ tsp chilli powder
¹/₂ tsp ground ginger
2 tsp mango powder
125 ml/4 fl oz natural yogurt
oil, for deep frying
4 poppadoms

1 Boil the chickpeas with the chilli in plenty of water for about 1 hour until tender, then drain.

2 Cut the potatoes into 2.5 cm/1 inch dice and mix into the chickpeas while they are still warm. Set aside.

3 Grind together the cumin, salt and peppercorns in a spice grinder or with a pestle and mortar. Stir in the mint, chilli powder, ginger and mango powder.

4 Put a small saucepan or frying pan over a low heat and add the spice mix. Stir until the spices give off their aroma and then immediately remove the pan from the heat.

5 Stir half of the spice mix into the chickpea and potato mixture and stir the other half into the yogurt.

6 Cook the poppadoms according to the packet instructions. Drain on plenty of kitchen paper. Break into bite-size pieces and stir into the potatoes and chickpeas, spoon over the spiced yogurt and serve immediately.

NUTRITION
Calories 262; Sugars 6 g; Protein 13 g;
Carbohydrate 46 g; Fat 4 g; Saturates 0.5 g

✪✪✪   moderate
     8 hrs 35 mins
        1 hr 5 mins

🍲 **COOK'S TIP**

Instead of chickpeas, diced tropical fruits can be stirred into the potatoes and spice mix; add a little lemon juice to balance the sweetness.

This is just one version of many dhals that are served throughout India; as many people are vegetarian, dhals form a staple part of the diet.

Tarka Dhal

1 Heat half of the ghee in a large saucepan and add the shallots. Cook for 2–3 minutes over a high heat, then add the mustard seeds. Cover the pan until the seeds begin to pop.

2 Immediately remove the lid from the pan and add the garlic, fenugreek, ginger and salt.

3 Stir once and add the lentils, tomato purée and water. Bring to the boil, then lower the heat and simmer the mixture gently for 10 minutes.

4 Stir in the tomatoes, lemon juice, and chopped coriander and simmer for 4–5 minutes until the lentils are tender.

5 Transfer to a serving dish. Heat the remaining ghee in a pan. Remove from the heat and stir in the garam masala and chilli powder. Pour over the tarka dhal and serve.

SERVES 4

2 tbsp ghee
2 shallots, sliced
1 tsp yellow mustard seeds
2 garlic cloves, crushed
8 fenugreek seeds
1 tsp grated fresh root ginger
$\frac{1}{2}$ tsp salt
125 g/4$\frac{1}{2}$ oz red lentils, washed
1 tbsp tomato purée
600 ml/1 pint water
2 tomatoes, peeled and chopped
1 tbsp lemon juice
4 tbsp chopped fresh coriander
$\frac{1}{2}$ tsp garam masala
$\frac{1}{2}$ tsp chilli powder

NUTRITION
Calories *183*; Sugars *4 g*; Protein *8 g*;
Carbohydrate *22 g*; Fat *8 g*; Saturates *5 g*

easy

10 mins

25 mins

🍴 **COOK'S TIP**

The flavours in a dhal can be altered to suit your particular taste; for example, for extra heat, add more chilli powder or chillies, or add fennel seeds for a pleasant aniseed flavour.

Dried pulses and lentils can be cooked in similar ways, but the soaking and cooking times do vary, so check the pack for instructions.

Toovar Dhal

SERVES 6

2 tbsp vegetable ghee
1 large onion, chopped finely
1 garlic clove, crushed
1 tbsp grated fresh root ginger
1 tbsp cumin seeds, ground
2 tsp coriander seeds, ground
1 dried red chilli
2.5 cm/1 inch piece of cinnamon stick
1 tsp salt
¹/₂ tsp ground turmeric
225 g/8 oz split yellow peas, soaked in cold water for 1 hour and drained
400 g/14 oz canned plum tomatoes
300 ml/10 fl oz water
2 tsp garam masala

1 Heat the ghee in a large saucepan, add the onion, garlic and ginger and fry for 3–4 minutes until the onion has softened slightly.

2 Add the cumin, coriander, chilli, cinnamon, salt and turmeric, then stir in the split peas until well mixed.

3 Add the tomatoes, with their can juices, breaking up the tomatoes slightly with the back of a spoon.

4 Add the water and bring to the boil. Reduce the heat to very low and simmer the dhal, uncovered, stirring occasionally, for about 40 minutes until most of the liquid has been absorbed and the split peas are tender. Skim the surface occasionally with a slotted spoon to remove any scum.

5 Gradually stir in the garam masala, tasting after each addition, until it is to your taste. Serve hot.

NUTRITION
Calories 195; Sugars 4 g; Protein 11 g;
Carbohydrate 28 g; Fat 5 g; Saturates 3 g

 easy

1hr 10 mins

50 mins

👑 **COOK'S TIP**

Use a non-stick saucepan if you have one, because the mixture is quite dense and does stick to the base of the pan occasionally. If the dhal is overstirred, the split peas will break up and the dish will not have much texture or bite.

Traditionally, koftas are made from a spicy meat mixture, but this bean and wheat version makes a tasty vegetarian alternative.

Kofta Kebabs

1 Cook the aduki beans in boiling water for 40 minutes, until tender. Drain, rinse and leave to cool. Cook the bulgur wheat in the stock for 10 minutes, until the stock is absorbed. Set aside.

2 Heat 1 tablespoon of the oil in a frying pan and fry the onion, garlic and spices for 4–5 minutes.

3 Transfer to a bowl, together with the beans, coriander, seasoning and eggs and mash with a potato masher or fork. Add the breadcrumbs and bulgur wheat and stir well to combine. Cover and chill for 1 hour, until firm.

4 To make the tabbouleh, soak the bulgur wheat in 425 ml/15 fl oz of boiling water for 15 minutes or until all the water has been absorbed. Combine with the remaining ingredients, then cover and chill until required.

5 With wet hands, mould the kofta mixture into 32 oval shapes.

6 Press on to skewers, brush with oil and grill for 5–6 minutes until golden. Turn, brush with oil again and cook for 5–6 minutes. Drain on kitchen paper. Garnish and serve with the tabbouleh.

SERVES 4

175 g/6 oz aduki beans
175 g/6 oz bulgur wheat
450 ml/16 fl oz Fresh Vegetable Stock
  (see page 16)
3 tbsp olive oil, plus extra for brushing
1 onion, chopped finely
2 garlic cloves, crushed
1 tsp ground coriander
1 tsp ground cumin
2 tbsp chopped fresh coriander
3 eggs, beaten
125 g/4½ oz dried breadcrumbs
salt and pepper

tabbouleh
175 g/6 oz bulgur wheat
2 tbsp lemon juice
1 tbsp olive oil
6 tbsp chopped fresh parsley
4 spring onions, chopped finely
60 g/2 oz finely chopped cucumber
3 tbsp chopped mint
1 extra-large tomato, chopped finely

NUTRITION
Calories *598*; Sugars *7 g*; Protein *26 g*;
Carbohydrate *90 g*; Fat *17 g*; Saturates *3 g*

 moderate
 1 hr 20 mins
1 hr 25 mins

Stir-fries *and* Sautés

Stir-frying is one of the most convenient and nutritious ways of cooking vegetarian food as ingredients are cooked quickly over a very high heat in very little oil. The high heat seals in the natural juices and helps preserve nutrients. The short cooking time makes the vegetables more succulent and preserves texture as well as the natural flavour and colour. A round-bottomed wok is ideal for stir-frying as it conducts and retains heat evenly and requires the use of less oil. You need a flat-bottomed pan for sautéing so that the food can be easily tossed and stirred. A brisk heat is essential so that the food turns golden brown and crisp.

This colourful and interesting mixture of vegetables, cooked in a spicy sauce, is excellent served with rice and naan bread.

Vegetable Curry

SERVES 4

225 g/8 oz turnips or swede
1 aubergine
350 g/12 oz new potatoes
225 g/8 oz cauliflower
225 g/8 oz button mushrooms
1 large onion
3 carrots
6 tbsp vegetable ghee or vegetable oil
2 garlic cloves, crushed
4 tsp finely chopped fresh root ginger
1–2 fresh green chillies, deseeded and chopped
1 tbsp paprika
2 tsp ground coriander
1 tbsp mild or medium curry powder
450 ml/16 fl oz Fresh Vegetable Stock
    (see page 16)
400 g/14 oz canned chopped tomatoes
1 green pepper, halved, deseeded and sliced
1 tbsp cornflour
150 ml/5 fl oz coconut milk
2–3 tbsp ground almonds
salt
fresh coriander sprigs, to garnish

NUTRITION
Calories 421; Sugars 20 g; Protein 12 g;
Carbohydrate 42 g; Fat 24 g; Saturates 3 g

easy

10 mins

45 mins

1 Cut the turnips or swede, aubergine and potatoes into 1-cm/1/2-inch cubes. Divide the cauliflower into small florets. Leave the mushrooms whole or slice them thickly if preferred. Slice the onion and carrots.

2 Heat the ghee or oil in a large pan. Add the onion, turnip or swede, potato and cauliflower and cook over a low heat, stirring frequently, for 3 minutes.

3 Add the garlic, ginger, chillies, paprika, ground coriander and curry powder and cook, stirring, for 1 minute.

4 Add the stock, tomatoes, aubergine and mushrooms and season with salt. Cover and simmer, stirring occasionally, for about 30 minutes or until tender. Add the green pepper and carrots, cover and cook for a further 5 minutes.

5 Blend the cornflour with the coconut milk to a smooth paste and stir into the mixture. Add the ground almonds and simmer, stirring constantly, for 2 minutes. Taste and adjust the seasoning if necessary. Transfer to serving plates and serve hot, garnished with coriander sprigs.

Meat is expensive in India and much of the population is vegetarian, so the cuisine is typified by tasty ways of cooking with vegetables.

Potato *and* Vegetable Curry

1 Heat the vegetable oil in a large heavy-based saucepan or frying pan. Add the potato chunks, onions and garlic and fry over a low heat, stirring frequently, for 2–3 minutes.

2 Add the garam masala, turmeric, ground cumin, ground coriander, ginger and chilli to the pan, mixing the spices into the vegetables until they are well coated. Fry over a low heat, stirring constantly, for 1 minute.

3 Add the cauliflower florets, tomatoes, peas, chopped fresh coriander and vegetable stock to the curry mixture.

4 Cook the potato curry over a low heat for 30–40 minutes or until the potatoes are tender and completely cooked through.

5 Garnish the potato curry with fresh coriander and serve with plain boiled rice or warm Indian bread.

SERVES 4

4 tbsp vegetable oil
675 g/1 lb 8 oz waxy potatoes, cut into large chunks
2 onions, quartered
3 garlic cloves, crushed
1 tsp garam masala
½ tsp ground turmeric
½ tsp ground cumin
½ tsp ground coriander
2 tsp grated fresh root ginger
1 fresh red chilli, chopped
225 g/8 oz cauliflower florets
4 tomatoes, peeled and quartered
75 g/2¾ oz frozen peas
2 tbsp chopped fresh coriander
300 ml/10 fl oz Fresh Vegetable Stock (see page 16)
shredded fresh coriander, to garnish
boiled rice or warm Indian bread, to serve

NUTRITION

Calories *301*; Sugars *10 g*; Protein *9 g*; Carbohydrate *41 g*; Fat *12 g*; Saturates *1 g*

  easy

 15 mins

 40–45 mins

Paneer is a delicious fresh, soft cheese frequently used in Indian cooking. It is easily made at home, but must be made the day before it's required.

Muttar Paneer

SERVES 4

150 ml/5 fl oz vegetable oil
2 onions, chopped
2 garlic cloves, crushed
2.5-cm/1-inch piece of fresh root ginger, chopped
1 tsp garam masala
1 tsp ground turmeric
1 tsp chilli powder
500 g/1 lb 2 oz frozen peas
225 g/8 oz can chopped tomatoes
125 ml/4 fl oz Fresh Vegetable Stock (see page 16)
salt and pepper
2 tbsp chopped coriander

paneer
2.5 litres/4½ pints milk
5 tbsp lemon juice
1 garlic clove, crushed (optional)
1 tbsp chopped fresh coriander (optional)

NUTRITION
Calories 550; Sugars 25 g; Protein 19 g; Carbohydrate 33 g; Fat 39 g; Saturates 12 g

★★★   moderate
🕐   8 hrs
🕐   30 mins

1 To make the paneer, bring the milk to a rolling boil in a large saucepan. Remove from the heat and stir in the lemon juice. Return to the heat for about 1 minute until the curds and whey separate. Remove from the heat. Line a colander with a double thickness of muslin and pour the mixture through the muslin, adding the garlic and coriander, if using. Squeeze all the liquid from the curds and leave to drain.

2 Transfer the muslin to a dish, cover with a plate and a heavy weight and leave overnight in the refrigerator.

3 Cut the pressed paneer into small cubes. Heat the oil in a large frying pan. Add the paneer and fry until golden on all sides. Remove from the pan and drain on kitchen paper.

4 Pour off some of the oil, leaving about 4 tablespoons in the pan. Add the onions, garlic and ginger and fry gently, stirring frequently, for 5 minutes. Stir in the spices and fry gently for 2 minutes. Add the peas, tomatoes and stock and season with salt and pepper. Cover and simmer, stirring occasionally, for 10 minutes, until the onion is tender.

5 Add the fried paneer cubes and cook for a further 5 minutes. Taste and adjust the seasoning, if necessary. Sprinkle with the fresh coriander and serve at once.

This vegetarian tomato curry is served topped with a few hard-boiled eggs. It is a lovely accompaniment to any Indian meal.

Tomato Curry

1 Place the tomatoes in a large mixing bowl. Add the ginger, garlic, chilli powder, salt, ground coriander and ground cumin and blend well.

2 Heat the oil in a saucepan. Add the onion, mustard, fenugreek and white cumin seeds, and the dried red chillies, and stir-fry for about 1 minute, until they give off their aroma. Remove the pan from the heat.

3 Add the tomato mixture to the spicy oil mixture and return the pan to the heat. Stir-fry for about 3 minutes.

4 Reduce the heat and continue to cook, half covered with a lid, stirring frequently, for 7–10 minutes.

5 Sprinkle over 1 tablespoon of the lemon juice. Taste, and add the remaining lemon juice if required.

6 Transfer the tomato curry to a warmed serving dish, set aside and keep warm until required.

7 Shell the hard-boiled eggs and cut them into quarters. Add them to the tomato curry, pushing them in gently, yolk end downwards. Serve hot.

SERVES 4

400 g/14 oz canned tomatoes
1 tsp finely chopped fresh root ginger
1 tsp crushed garlic
1 tsp chilli powder
1 tsp salt
$\frac{1}{2}$ tsp ground coriander
$\frac{1}{2}$ tsp ground cumin
4 tbsp oil
$\frac{1}{2}$ tsp onion seeds
$\frac{1}{2}$ tsp mustard seeds
$\frac{1}{2}$ tsp fenugreek seeds
pinch of white cumin seeds
3 dried red chillies
2 tbsp lemon juice
3 eggs, hard-boiled
fresh coriander leaves, to garnish

NUTRITION
Calories 170; Sugars 3 g; Protein 6 g; Carbohydrate 3 g; Fat 15 g; Saturates 2 g

✿✿✿   moderate
    25 mins
    15 mins

Green curry paste will keep for up to three weeks in the refrigerator. Serve the curry over rice or noodles.

Green Curry *with* Tempeh

SERVES 4

1 tbsp sunflower oil
175 g/6 oz marinated or plain tempeh,
   cut into diamonds
6 spring onions, cut into 2.5-cm/1-inch pieces
150 ml/¼ pint coconut milk
grated rind of 1 lime
15 g/½ oz fresh basil leaves
¼ tsp liquid seasoning

green curry paste
2 tsp coriander seeds
1 tsp cumin seeds
1 tsp black peppercorns
4 large green chillies, deseeded and chopped
2 shallots, quartered
2 garlic cloves,
grated rind of 1 lime
1 tbsp roughly chopped galangal
1 tsp ground turmeric
salt
2 tbsp oil
2 tbsp chopped fresh coriander, plus leaves,
   to garnish

NUTRITION

Calories 237; Sugars 4 g; Protein 16 g;
Carbohydrate 5 g; Fat 17 g; Saturates 3 g

moderate

20 mins

15–20 mins

1 To make the green curry paste, grind together the coriander, cumin seeds and black peppercorns in a food processor or with a mortar and pestle.

2 Blend the remaining ingredients together and add the ground spice mixture. The curry paste can be stored in a clean, dry jar for up to 3 weeks in the refrigerator, or it can be frozen in a suitable container.

3 For the curry, heat the oil in a wok or large, heavy frying pan. Add the tempeh and stir over a high heat for about 2 minutes until sealed on all sides. Add the spring onions and stir-fry for 1 minute. Remove the tempeh and spring onions and reserve.

4 Put half the coconut milk into the wok or pan and bring to the boil. Add 6 tablespoons of the curry paste and the lime rind, and cook for 1 minute, until fragrant. Add the reserved tempeh and spring onions.

5 Add the remaining coconut milk and simmer for about 7–8 minutes. Stir in the fresh basil leaves and liquid seasoning. Leave the curry to simmer for a further minute before serving, garnished with coriander leaves and chillies.

This rice is colourful and satisfyingly crunchy with the addition of sweetcorn and red kidney beans.

Fried Rice *with* Spicy Beans

1 Heat the sunflower oil in a large preheated wok.

2 Add the onion and stir-fry over a medium heat for about 2 minutes or until softened.

3 Lower the heat, add the rice, green pepper and chilli powder to the wok and stir-fry for 1 minute.

4 Pour in the boiling water. Bring back to the boil, then reduce the heat and simmer for 15 minutes.

5 Stir in the sweetcorn, kidney beans and coriander and heat through, stirring from time to time.

6 Transfer to a warmed serving bowl and serve hot, sprinkled with extra coriander, if wished.

SERVES 4

3 tbsp sunflower oil
1 onion, finely chopped
225 g/8 oz long grain rice
1 green pepper, halved, deseeded and diced
1 tsp chilli powder
600 ml/1 pint boiling water
100 g/3½ oz canned sweetcorn kernels
225 g/8 oz canned red kidney beans, drained and rinsed
2 tbsp chopped fresh coriander
chopped fresh coriander, (optional), to garnish

NUTRITION
Calories *363*; Sugars *3 g*; Protein *10 g*; Carbohydrate *61 g*; Fat *11 g*; Saturates *2 g*

 moderate

 15 mins

🕐 20 mins

🍳 COOK'S TIP

For perfect fried rice, the raw rice should ideally be soaked in a bowl of water for a short time before cooking to remove excess starch. Short grain Oriental rice can be substituted for the long grain rice.

VEGETARIAN

This tasty meal is made with sliced potatoes, tofu and vegetables cooked in the pan from which it is served.

Pan Potato Cake

SERVES 4

675 g/1 lb 8 oz waxy potatoes, unpeeled and sliced
1 carrot, diced
225 g/8 oz small broccoli florets
5 tbsp butter
2 tbsp vegetable oil
1 red onion, quartered
2 garlic cloves, crushed
175 g/6 oz firm tofu, diced
2 tbsp chopped fresh sage
85 g/3 oz mature Cheddar cheese, grated

1 Cook the sliced potatoes in a large saucepan of boiling water for 10 minutes. Drain thoroughly.

2 Meanwhile, cook the carrot and broccoli florets in a separate pan of boiling water for 5 minutes. Remove with a slotted spoon.

3 Heat the butter and oil in a 23-cm/9-inch frying pan. Add the onion and garlic and fry over a low heat for 2–3 minutes. Add half of the potato slices, covering the base of the pan.

4 Cover the potato slices with the carrot, broccoli and tofu. Sprinkle with half of the sage and cover with the remaining potato slices. Sprinkle the grated cheese over the top.

5 Cook over a moderate heat for 8–10 minutes. Then place the pan under a preheated medium grill for about 2–3 minutes, or until the cheese melts and browns.

6 Garnish with the remaining chopped sage and serve immediately, straight from the pan.

NUTRITION
Calories 452; Sugars 6 g; Protein 17 g; Carbohydrate 35 g; Fat 28 g; Saturates 13 g

easy
15 mins
30 mins

COOK'S TIP

Make sure that the mixture fills the whole width of your frying pan to enable the layers to remain intact.

This is a vegetarian version of chicken Kiev – the bean patties are topped with garlic and herb butter and coated in breadcrumbs.

Kidney Bean Kiev

1 To make the garlic butter, put the butter, garlic and parsley in a bowl and blend together with a wooden spoon. Place the garlic butter on to a sheet of baking parchment, roll into a cigar shape and wrap in the baking parchment. Chill in the refrigerator until required.

2 Using a potato masher, mash the red kidney beans in a mixing bowl and stir in 75 g/2¾ oz of the breadcrumbs, until thoroughly blended.

3 Melt the butter in a heavy-based frying pan. Add the leek and celery and sauté over a low heat, stirring constantly, for 3–4 minutes.

4 Add the bean mixture to the pan, together with the parsley, season with salt and pepper to taste and mix thoroughly. Remove the pan from the heat and set aside to cool slightly.

5 When cool, divide the kidney bean mixture into 4 equal portions and shape them into ovals.

6 Slice the garlic butter into 4 pieces and place a slice in the centre of each bean patty. With your hands, mould the bean mixture around the garlic butter to encase it completely.

7 Dip each bean patty into the beaten egg to coat and then roll in the remaining breadcrumbs.

8 Heat a little oil in a frying pan and fry the patties, turning once, for 7–10 minutes, or until golden brown. Serve immediately.

SERVES 4

garlic butter
100 g/3½ oz butter
3 garlic cloves, crushed
1 tbsp chopped fresh parsley

bean patties
675 g/1 lb 8 oz canned red kidney beans
150 g/5½ oz fresh white breadcrumbs
25 g/1 oz butter
1 leek, chopped
1 celery stick, chopped
1 tbsp chopped fresh parsley
1 egg, beaten
salt and pepper
vegetable oil, for shallow frying

NUTRITION
Calories *688*; Sugars *8 g*; Protein *17 g*;
Carbohydrate *49 g*; Fat *49 g*; Saturates *20 g*

moderate

25 mins

20 mins

Bubble and squeak is best known as fried mashed potato and left-over greens, served as an accompaniment. This version has tofu added.

Bubble *and* Squeak

SERVES 4

450 g/1 lb floury potatoes, diced
225 g/8 oz Savoy cabbage, shredded
5 tbsp vegetable oil
2 leeks, chopped
1 garlic clove, crushed
225 g/8 oz smoked tofu, cubed
salt and pepper
shredded cooked leek, to garnish

1 Cook the diced potatoes in a saucepan of lightly salted boiling water for 10 minutes, until tender. Drain and mash the potatoes.

2 Meanwhile, in a separate saucepan, blanch the cabbage in boiling water for 5 minutes. Drain well and add to the potato.

3 Heat the oil in a heavy-based frying pan. Add the leeks and garlic and fry gently for 2–3 minutes. Stir into the potato and cabbage mixture.

4 Add the smoked tofu and season well with salt and pepper. Cook over a moderate heat for 10 minutes.

5 Carefully turn the whole mixture over and continue to cook over a moderate heat for a further 5–7 minutes, until it is crispy underneath.

6 Serve immediately, garnished with shredded leek.

NUTRITION

Calories 301; Sugars 5 g; Protein 11 g;
Carbohydrate 24 g; Fat 18 g; Saturates 2 g

easy

15 mins

40 mins

🍳 **COOK'S TIP**

This is a perfect main meal, because the smoked tofu cubes added to the basic bubble and squeak mixture make it very substantial and nourishing.

The freshness of lightly cooked summer vegetables is enhanced by the aromatic flavour of a tarragon and white wine dressing.

Sauté *of* Summer Vegetables

1 Cut the carrots in half lengthways, slice the runner beans and courgettes, and halve the spring onions and radishes, so that all the vegetables are cut into even-sized pieces.

2 Melt the butter in a large, heavy-based frying pan or wok. Add all the vegetables and fry them over a medium heat, stirring frequently, until they are tender, but still crisp and firm to the bite.

3 Meanwhile, pour the olive oil, vinegar, and white wine into a small saucepan and add the sugar. Place over a low heat, stirring constantly until the sugar has dissolved. Remove the pan from the heat and add the chopped tarragon.

4 When the vegetables are just cooked, pour over the 'dressing'. Stir through, tossing the vegetables well to coat. Season to taste with salt and pepper and then transfer to a warmed serving dish.

5 Garnish with fresh tarragon sprigs and serve the sauté immediately.

SERVES 4

225 g/8 oz baby carrots, scrubbed
125 g/4½ oz runner beans
2 courgettes, trimmed
1 bunch of large spring onions
1 bunch of radishes
4 tbsp butter
2 tbsp light olive oil
2 tbsp white wine vinegar
4 tbsp dry white wine
1 tsp caster sugar
1 tbsp chopped fresh tarragon
salt and pepper
fresh tarragon sprigs, to garnish

NUTRITION

Calories 217; Sugars 8 g; Protein 2 g; Carbohydrate 9 g; Fat 18 g; Saturates 9 g

⭐ very easy

 10 mins

 10–15 mins

This vegetarian version
of paella is packed with
vegetables and nuts for
a truly delicious and
simple dish.

Cashew Nut Paella

SERVES 4

2 tbsp olive oil
1 tbsp butter
1 red onion, chopped
150 g/5½ oz arborio rice
1 tsp ground turmeric
1 tsp ground cumin
½ tsp chilli powder
3 garlic cloves, crushed
1 fresh green chilli, deseeded and sliced
1 green pepper, halved, deseeded and diced
1 red pepper, halved, deseeded and diced
85 g/3 oz baby corn cobs
2 tbsp stoned black olives
1 large tomato, deseeded and diced
450 ml/16 fl oz Fresh Vegetable Stock
    (see page 16)
85 g/3 oz unsalted cashew nuts
55 g/2 oz frozen peas
2 tbsp chopped fresh parsley
pinch of cayenne pepper
salt and pepper
fresh herbs, to garnish

NUTRITION

Calories 406; Sugars 8 g; Protein 10 g;
Carbohydrate 44 g; Fat 22 g; Saturates 6 g

easy

15 mins

35 mins

1 Heat the olive oil and butter in a large frying pan or paella pan until the butter has melted.

2 Add the onion and cook over a medium heat, stirring constantly, for 2–3 minutes until softened.

3 Stir in the rice, turmeric, cumin, chilli powder, garlic, sliced chilli, green and red peppers, corn cobs, olives and tomato and cook over a medium heat, stirring occasionally, for 1–2 minutes.

4 Pour in the stock and bring the mixture to the boil. Reduce the heat and cook gently, stirring constantly, for a further 20 minutes.

5 Add the cashew nuts and peas and continue to cook, stirring occasionally, for a further 5 minutes. Season to taste with salt and pepper and sprinkle with fresh chopped parsley and a pinch of cayenne pepper. Transfer the paella to warm serving plates, garnish with fresh herbs and serve immediately.

East meets West in this delicious dish. Prepare all the vegetables and cook the pasta in advance, then the dish can be cooked in a few minutes.

Vegetable Pasta Stir-fry

1 Cook the pasta in a large pan of boiling, lightly salted water, adding the tablespoon of olive oil. When tender, but still firm to the bite, drain the pasta in a colander, return to the pan, cover and keep warm.

2 Cook the carrots and baby corn cobs in boiling, salted water for 2 minutes. Drain in a colander, plunge into cold water to prevent further cooking and drain again.

3 Heat the peanut oil in a large frying pan over medium heat. Add the ginger and stir-fry for 1 minute, to flavour the oil. Remove the ginger with a slotted spoon and discard.

4 Add the onion, garlic, celery and peppers to the oil and stir-fry over a medium heat for 2 minutes. Add the carrots and baby corn cobs, and stir-fry for a further 2 minutes, then stir in the reserved pasta.

5 For the sauce, put the cornflour in a small bowl and mix to a smooth paste with the water. Stir in the soy sauce, the sherry and the honey.

6 Pour the sauce into the saucepan with the pasta, stir well and cook for 2 minutes, stirring once or twice. Taste the sauce and season with hot pepper sauce, if wished. Serve with a steamed green vegetable, such as mangetouts.

SERVES 4

400 g/14 oz dried wholewheat penne pasta
1 tbsp olive oil
2 carrots, sliced thinly
115 g/4 oz baby corn cobs
3 tbsp peanut oil
2.5-cm/1-inch piece fresh gingerroot, sliced
1 large onion, thinly sliced
1 garlic clove, thinly sliced
3 celery sticks, thinly sliced
1 small red pepper, halved, deseeded and sliced into matchstick strips
1 small green pepper, deseeded and sliced into matchstick strips
salt
steamed mangetout, to serve

s a u c e
1 tsp cornflour
2 tbsp water
3 tbsp soy sauce
3 tbsp dry sherry
1 tsp clear honey
dash of hot pepper sauce (optional)

NUTRITION
Calories *383*; Sugars *18 g*; Protein *14 g*;
Carbohydrate *32 g*; Fat *23 g*; Saturates *8 g*

⭐⭐   easy
        20 mins
        25 mins

Serve this dish with plain noodles or fluffy white rice for a filling and flavoursome oriental meal.

Sweet *and* Sour Vegetables

SERVES 4

1 tbsp peanut oil
2 garlic cloves, crushed
1 tsp grated fresh root ginger
50 g/1¾ oz baby corn cobs
50 g/1¾ oz mangetout
1 carrot, cut into matchsticks
1 green pepper, halved, deseeded and
    cut into matchsticks
8 spring onions
50 g/1¾ oz canned bamboo shoots
225 g/8 oz marinated firm tofu, cubed
2 tbsp dry sherry or Chinese rice wine
2 tbsp rice wine vinegar
2 tbsp clear honey
1 tbsp light soy sauce
150 ml/¼ 5 fl oz Fresh Vegetable Stock
    (see page 16)
1 tbsp cornflour
noodles or boiled rice, to serve

1 Heat the oil in a preheated wok until it is almost smoking. Add the garlic and the fresh root ginger and cook over a medium heat, stirring frequently, for 30 seconds.

2 Add the baby corn cobs, the mangetout and the carrot and pepper matchsticks and stir-fry for about 5 minutes, or until the vegetables are tender, but still crisp.

3 Add the spring onions, bamboo shoots and tofu and cook for 2 minutes.

4 Stir in the sherry or Chinese rice wine, the rice vinegar, honey, soy sauce, vegetable stock and cornflour and bring to the boil. Reduce the heat to low and simmer for 2 minutes, until heated through.

5 Transfer to warmed serving dishes and serve immediately.

NUTRITION
Calories *401*; Sugars *16 g*; Protein *14 g*;
Carbohydrate *70 g*; Fat *9 g*; Saturates *2 g*

          very easy
          10 mins
                  15 mins

Grated carrots, courgettes and feta cheese are combined with cumin seeds, poppy seeds, curry powder and fresh parsley in these little patties.

Feta Cheese Patties

1 Grate the carrots, courgette, onion and feta cheese coarsely, either by hand or process in a food processor.

2 Place the flour, cumin seeds, poppy seeds, curry powder and parsley in a large bowl and stir to combine. Season to taste with salt and pepper.

3 Add the vegetable and cheese mixture to the seasoned flour, tossing well to combine. Stir in the beaten egg.

4 Heat the butter and oil in a large, heavy-based frying pan. Place heaped tablespoonfuls of the patty mixture in the pan, flattening them slightly with the back of the spoon. Cook over a low heat, for about 2 minutes on each side, until crisp and golden brown. Drain on kitchen paper and keep warm. Cook more patties in the same way until all the mixture is used.

5 Serve immediately, garnished with fresh herbs sprigs.

SERVES 4

2 large carrots
1 large courgette
1 small onion
55 g/2 oz feta cheese
4 tbsp plain flour
¼ tsp cumin seeds
½ tsp poppy seeds
1 tsp medium curry powder
1 tbsp chopped fresh parsley
1 egg, beaten
2 tbsp butter
2 tbsp vegetable oil
salt and pepper
fresh herb sprigs, to garnish

NUTRITION
Calories 217; Sugars 6 g; Protein 6 g;
Carbohydrate 12 g; Fat 16 g; Saturates 7 g

 easy

 15 mins

20 mins

Casseroles *and* Bakes

Anyone who ever thought that vegetarian meals were dull will be proved wrong by the rich variety of dishes in this chapter. You'll recognize influences from Mexican and Chinese cooking, but there are also traditional stews and casseroles, as well as hearty bakes and roasts. They all make exciting meals, at any time of year, and for virtually any occasion. Don't be afraid to substitute your own personal favourite ingredients where appropriate. There is no reason why you cannot enjoy experimenting and adding your own touch to these imaginative ideas.

This is a really hearty dish, perfect for cold days when a filling hot meal is just what you need to keep the winter out.

Lentil *and* Rice Casserole

SERVES 4

225 g/8 oz split red lentils, washed
55 g/2 oz long grain rice
1.2 litres/2 pints Fresh Vegetable Stock
　(see page 16)
1 leek, cut into chunks
3 garlic cloves, crushed
400 g/14 oz canned chopped tomatoes
1 tsp ground cumin
1 tsp chilli powder
1 tsp garam masala
1 red pepper, halved, deseeded and sliced
100 g/3½ oz small broccoli florets
8 baby corn cobs, halved lengthways
55 g/2 oz French beans, halved
1 tbsp shredded fresh basil
salt and pepper
fresh basil sprigs, to garnish

1 Place the lentils, rice and vegetable stock in a large flameproof casserole and cook over a low heat, stirring occasionally, for 20 minutes.

2 Add the leek, garlic, tomatoes and their can juice, ground cumin, chilli powder, garam masala, sliced pepper, broccoli, corn cobs and French beans to the pan.

3 Bring the mixture to the boil, reduce the heat, cover and simmer for a further 10–15 minutes or until the vegetables are tender.

4 Add the shredded basil and season with salt and pepper to taste.

5 Garnish with fresh basil sprigs and serve immediately.

NUTRITION

Calories 312; Sugars 9 g; Protein 20 g;
Carbohydrate 51 g; Fat 2 g; Saturates 0.4 g

moderate

15 mins

20 mins

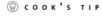 **COOK'S TIP**

You can vary the rice in this recipe – use brown or wild rice, if you prefer.

Seasonal fresh vegetables are casseroled with lentils, then topped with a ring of fresh cheese scones to make this tasty cobbler.

Winter Vegetable Cobbler

1 Heat the oil and cook the garlic and onions for 5 minutes. Add the celery, swede, carrots and cauliflower and cook for 2–3 minutes. Add the mushrooms, tomatoes and lentils. Mix the cornflour and water and stir into the pan with the stock, Tabasco and oregano.

2 Transfer to an ovenproof dish, cover and bake in a preheated oven, 180°C/350°F/Gas Mark 4, for 20 minutes.

3 To make the topping, sift the flour with a pinch of salt into a bowl. Rub in the butter, then stir in most of the cheese and the oregano. Beat the egg with the milk and add enough to the dry ingredients to make a soft dough. Knead lightly, roll out to 1-cm/½-inch thick and cut into 5-cm/2-inch rounds.

4 Remove the dish from the oven and increase the temperature to 200°C/400°F/Gas Mark 6. Arrange the scones around the edge of the dish, brush with the remaining egg and milk and sprinkle with the reserved cheese. Cook for a further 10–12 minutes. Garnish and serve.

SERVES 4

1 tbsp olive oil
1 garlic clove, crushed
8 small onions, halved
2 celery sticks, sliced
225 g/8 oz swede, chopped
2 carrots, sliced
½ small cauliflower, broken into florets
225 g/8 oz mushrooms, sliced
400 g/14 oz canned chopped tomatoes
55 g/2 oz red lentils, washed
2 tbsp cornflour
3–4 tbsp water
300 ml/10 fl oz Fresh Vegetable Stock
   (see page 16)
2 tsp Tabasco sauce
2 tsp chopped oregano, plus sprigs to garnish

cobbler topping
225 g/8 oz self-raising flour
4 tbsp butter
115 g/4 oz grated mature Cheddar cheese
2 tsp chopped fresh oregano
1 egg, lightly beaten
150 ml/5 fl oz milk
salt

NUTRITION
Calories 734; Sugars 22 g; Protein 27 g;
Carbohydrate 96 g; Fat 30 g; Saturates 16 g

✪✪✪   moderate
   20 mins
   40 mins

The perfect dish to serve for Sunday lunch. Roast vegetables make a succulent accompaniment.

Lentil Roast

SERVES 4

225 g/8 oz red lentils, washed
450 ml/16 fl oz Fresh Vegetable Stock (see page 16)
1 bay leaf
15 g/½ oz butter or margarine, softened
2 tbsp dried wholemeal breadcrumbs
225 g/8 oz grated mature Cheddar cheese
1 leek, chopped finely
125 g/4½ oz button mushrooms, chopped finely
90 g/3¼ oz fresh wholemeal breadcrumbs
2 tbsp chopped fresh parsley
1 tbsp lemon juice
2 eggs, lightly beaten
salt and pepper
fresh flat-leaf parsley sprigs, to garnish
mixed roast vegetables, to serve

1 Put the lentils, stock and bay leaf in a saucepan. Bring to the boil, cover and simmer gently for 15–20 minutes, until all the liquid is absorbed and the lentils have softened. Discard the bay leaf.

2 Base-line a 1 kg/2 lb 4 oz loaf tin with baking parchment. Grease with the butter or margarine and sprinkle with the dried breadcrumbs.

3 Stir the grated cheese, chopped leek and mushrooms, fresh breadcrumbs and parsley into the lentils.

4 Bind the mixture together with the lemon juice and eggs. Season with salt and pepper. Spoon into the prepared loaf tin and smooth the top. Bake in a preheated oven, 190°C/ 375°F/Gas Mark 5, for about 1 hour, until golden.

5 Loosen the loaf with a palette knife and turn onto a warmed serving plate. Slice, garnish with parsley and serve, with mixed roast vegetables.

NUTRITION
Calories 400; Sugars 2 g; Protein 26 g;
Carbohydrate 32 g; Fat 20 g; Saturates 10 g

 challenging

🕐 15 mins

🕐 1 hr 20 mins

Toasted almonds are combined with sesame seeds, rice and vegetables in this tasty roast. Serve it with a delicious onion and mushroom sauce.

Almond *and* Sesame Roast

1 Heat the oil in a large frying pan and cook the onion gently for 2–3 minutes. Add the rice and cook gently for 5–6 minutes, stirring frequently.

2 Add the stock, bring to the boil, lower the heat and simmer for 15 minutes or until the rice is tender. Add a little extra water if necessary. Remove from the heat and transfer to a large mixing bowl.

3 Add the carrot, leek, sesame seeds, almonds, cheese, beaten eggs and herbs. Mix well and season with salt and pepper to taste. Transfer the mixture to a greased 500 g/1 lb 2 oz loaf tin, smoothing the surface. Bake in a preheated oven, 180°C/ 350°F/Gas Mark 4, for 1 hour until set and firm. Leave in the tin for 10 minutes.

4 To make the sauce, melt the butter in a small pan and cook the onion until dark golden brown. Add the mushrooms and cook for 2 minutes. Stir in the flour, cook gently for 1 minute, then gradually add the stock. Bring to the boil, stirring constantly, until thickened and blended. Season to taste with salt and pepper.

5 Turn out the nut roast, slice and serve, garnished with parsley sprigs, with fresh vegetables, accompanied by the onion and mushroom sauce.

SERVES 4

2 tbsp sesame or olive oil
1 small onion, chopped finely
55 g/2 oz risotto rice
300 ml/10 fl oz Fresh Vegetable Stock (see page 16)
1 large carrot, grated
1 large leek, chopped finely
2 tsp sesame seeds, toasted
85 g/3 oz chopped almonds, toasted
55 g/2 oz ground almonds
85 g/3 oz grated mature Cheddar cheese
2 eggs, beaten
1 tsp mixed dried herbs
butter, for greasing
salt and pepper
fresh flat-leaf parsley sprigs, to garnish
fresh vegetables, to serve

sauce

2 tbsp butter
1 small onion, chopped finely
115 g/4 oz finely chopped mushrooms
4 tbsp plain flour
300 ml/10 fl oz Fresh Vegetable S tock (see page 16)

NUTRITION

Calories *612*; Sugars *7 g*; Protein *22 g*; Carbohydrate *29 g*; Fat *46 g*; Saturates *13 g*

✪✪✪   moderate
🕐   20–30 mins
🕐   1 hr 30 mins

VEGETARIAN

A wonderful mixture of red lentils, tofu and vegetables is cooked beneath a crunchy potato topping for a really hearty meal.

Potato-Topped Lentil Bake

SERVES 4

topping
675 g/1 lb 8 oz floury potatoes, diced
25 g/1 oz butter
1 tbsp milk
50 g/1³/₄ oz chopped pecan nuts
2 tbsp chopped fresh thyme
fresh thyme sprigs, to garnish

filling
225 g/8 oz red lentils, washed
55 g/2 oz butter
1 leek, sliced
2 garlic cloves, crushed
1 celery stick, chopped
125 g/4¹/₂ oz broccoli florets
175 g/6 oz smoked tofu, cubed
2 tsp tomato purée
salt and pepper

NUTRITION
Calories 627; Sugars 7 g; Protein 26 g;
Carbohydrate 66 g; Fat 30 g; Saturates 13 g

moderate

10 mins

1 hr 30 mins

1 To make the topping, cook the diced potatoes in a saucepan of boiling water for 10–15 minutes, or until cooked through. Drain well, add the butter and milk and mash thoroughly. Stir in the choped pecan nuts and the chopped thyme and set aside.

2 Cook the lentils in boiling water for 20–30 minutes, or until tender. Drain and set aside.

3 Melt the butter in a frying pan. Add the leek, garlic, celery and broccoli. Fry over a medium heat, stirring frequently, for 5 minutes, until softened.

4 Add the tofu cubes. Stir in the lentils, together with the tomato purée. Season with salt and pepper to taste, then turn the mixture into the base of a shallow ovenproof dish.

5 Spoon the mashed potato on top of the lentil mixture, spreading to cover it completely.

6 Cook the lentil bake in a preheated oven, 200°C/400°F/Gas Mark 6, for about 30–35 minutes, or until the topping is golden brown. Remove the bake from the oven, garnish with fresh thyme sprigs and serve hot.

🍲 **COOK'S TIP**

You can use almost any combination of your favourite vegetables in this dish.

This bake of sweetcorn and kidney beans, flavoured with chilli and fresh coriander, is topped with crispy cheese cornbread.

Mexican Chilli Corn Pie

1 Heat the oil in a large frying pan and gently fry the garlic, peppers and celery for 5–6 minutes until just softened.

2 Stir in the chilli powder, tomatoes and sweetcorn. Rinse the beans and add to the mixture with seasoning. Bring to the boil and simmer for 10 minutes. Stir in the coriander and spoon into an ovenproof dish.

3 To make the topping, mix together the cornmeal, flour and baking powder. Make a well in the centre, add the egg, milk and oil and beat until a smooth batter is formed.

4 Spoon the corn mixture over the pepper and sweetcorn and sprinkle with the cheese. Bake in a preheated oven, at 220°C/425°F/Gas Mark 7, for 25–30 minutes until golden and firm.

5 Garnish with coriander sprigs and serve immediately with a tomato and avocado salad.

SERVES 4

1 tbsp corn oil
2 garlic cloves, crushed
1 red pepper, halved, deseeded and diced
1 green pepper, halved, deseeded and diced
1 celery stick, diced
1 tsp hot chilli powder
400 g/14 oz canned chopped tomatoes
325 g/11½ oz canned sweetcorn kernels, drained
215 g/7½ oz canned kidney beans, drained
2 tbsp chopped fresh coriander
salt and pepper
fresh coriander sprigs, to garnish
tomato and avocado salad, to serve

topping
125 g/4½ oz cornmeal
1 tbsp plain flour
2 tsp baking powder
1 egg, beaten
6 tbsp milk
1 tbsp corn oil
125 g/4½ oz grated mature Cheddar cheese

NUTRITION
Calories 519; Sugars 17 g; Protein 22 g;
Carbohydrate 61 g; Fat 22 g; Saturates 9 g

✪✪✪   moderate
   25 mins
   45 mins

In this recipe, a variety of vegetables are cooked under a layer of potatoes, topped with cheese and cooked until golden brown.

Vegetable Hotpot

SERVES 4

600 g/1 lb 5 oz potatoes, thinly sliced
2 tbsp vegetable oil
1 red onion, halved and sliced
1 leek, sliced
2 garlic cloves, crushed
1 carrot, cut into chunks
100 g/3½ oz broccoli florets
100 g/3½ oz cauliflower florets
2 small turnips, quartered
1 tbsp plain flour
700 ml/1¼ pints Fresh Vegetable Stock
   (see page 16)
150 ml/5 fl oz dry cider
1 eating apple, cored and sliced
2 tbsp chopped fresh sage
pinch of cayenne pepper
50 g/1¾ oz Cheddar cheese, grated
salt and pepper

1 Cook the potato slices in a saucepan of boiling water for 10 minutes. Drain thoroughly and reserve.

2 Heat the vegetable oil in a flameproof casserole. Add the onion, leek and garlic to the oil and sauté, stirring occasionally, for 2–3 minutes.

3 Add the remaining vegetables and cook, stirring constantly, for a further 3–4 minutes.

4 Stir in the flour and cook for 1 minute. Gradually add the vegetable stock and cider and bring to the boil. Add the apple, sage and cayenne pepper and season well with salt and pepper.

5 Remove from the heat and transfer the vegetables to an ovenproof dish.

6 Arrange the potato slices on top of the vegetable mixture to cover.

7 Sprinkle the grated cheese on top of the potato slices and cook in a preheated oven, 190°C/375°F/Gas Mark 5, for about 30–35 minutes or until the potato is golden brown and beginning to crispen around the edges. Serve the vegetable hotpot immediately, straight from the dish.

NUTRITION
Calories 279; Sugars 12 g; Protein 10 g;
Carbohydrate 34 g; Fat 11 g; Saturates 4 g

easy

25 mins

1 hr

A tasty, simple supper dish of choux pastry and crisp green vegetables. The choux pastry ring can be filled with all kinds of vegetables.

Green Vegetable Gougère

1 Sift the flour on to a piece of baking parchment. Cut the butter into dice and put in a saucepan with the water. Heat until the butter has melted. Bring the butter and water to the boil, then tip in the flour all at once. Beat until the mixture becomes thick. Remove from the heat and continue to beat until the mixture is glossy and comes away from the sides of the saucepan.

2 Transfer to a mixing bowl and cool for 10 minutes. Gradually beat in the eggs, a little at a time, making sure they are thoroughly incorporated after each addition. Stir in 55 g/2 oz of the cheese and season with salt and pepper.

3 Place spoonfuls of the mixture in a 23-cm/9-inch circle on a dampened baking tray. Brush with milk and sprinkle with the remaining cheese.

4 Bake in a preheated oven, 220°C/425°F/Gas Mark 7, for 30–35 minutes, until golden and crisp. Transfer to a warmed serving plate.

5 Meanwhile, make the filling. Heat the butter or margarine and the olive oil in a large frying pan and stir-fry the leeks and cabbage for 2 minutes. Add the beansprouts, lime rind and juice and stir-fry for 1 minute. Season to taste with celery salt and pepper.

6 Pile into the centre of the pastry ring. Garnish with lime slices and serve.

S E R V E S   4

150 g/5½ oz plain flour
125 g/4½ oz butter
300 ml/10 fl oz water
4 eggs, beaten
90 g/3¼ oz grated Gruyère cheese
1 tbsp milk
salt and pepper

filling

2 tbsp garlic and herb butter or margarine
2 tsp olive oil
2 leeks, shredded
225 g/8 oz green cabbage, finely shredded
125 g/4½ oz beansprouts
½ tsp grated lime rind
1 tbsp lime juice
celery salt and pepper
lime slices, to garnish

N U T R I T I O N
Calories *672*; Sugars *6 g*; Protein *19 g*;
Carbohydrate *36 g*; Fat *51 g*; Saturates *14 g*

moderate

30 mins

40 mins

These strudels look really impressive and are perfect for a casual supper or served as a more formal dinner party dish.

Vegetable *and* Tofu Strudels

SERVES 4

filling
2 tbsp vegetable oil
2 tbsp butter
150 g/5½ oz potatoes, finely diced
1 leek, shredded
2 garlic cloves, crushed
1 tsp garam masala
½ tsp chilli powder
½ tsp turmeric
50 g/1¾ oz okra, sliced
100 g/3½ oz button mushrooms, sliced
2 tomatoes, diced
225 g/8 oz firm tofu, diced
salt and pepper

pastry
350 g/12 oz (12 sheets) filo pastry
2 tbsp butter, melted

1 To make the filling, heat the oil and butter in a frying pan. Add the potatoes and leek and fry, stirring constantly, for 2–3 minutes.

2 Add the garlic and spices, okra, mushrooms, tomatoes and tofu and season to taste with salt and pepper. Cook, stirring, for 5–7 minutes, or until tender.

3 Lay the pastry out on a chopping board and brush each individual sheet with melted butter. Place 3 sheets on top of one another; repeat to make 4 stacks.

4 Spoon a quarter of the filling along the centre of each stack and brush the edges with melted butter. Fold the short edges in and roll up lengthways to form a cigar shape. Brush the outside with melted butter. Place the strudels on a greased baking tray.

5 Cook in a preheated oven, 190°C/ 375°F/Gas Mark 5, for 20 minutes, or until golden brown and crisp. Transfer the strudels to a warm serving dish and serve them immediately.

NUTRITION
Calories *485*; Sugars *5 g*; Protein *16 g*;
Carbohydrate *47 g*; Fat *27 g*; Saturates *5 g*

moderate

25 mins

30 mins

These puff pastry parcels, filled with garlic, mushrooms and spinach, are easy to make and simply melt in the mouth.

Mushroom *and* Spinach Puffs

1 Melt the butter in a frying pan. Add the onion and garlic and sauté over a low heat, stirring, for 3–4 minutes, until the onion has softened.

2 Add the mushrooms, spinach and nutmeg and cook over a medium heat, stirring occasionally, for 2–3 minutes.

3 Stir in the double cream, stirring to combine thoroughly. Season with salt and pepper to taste and remove the pan from the heat.

4 Roll the pastry out on a lightly floured surface and cut into four 15-cm/ 6-inch rounds.

5 Put a quarter of the filling on to 1 half of each round and fold the pastry over to encase it.

6 Press down to seal the edges and brush with the beaten egg. Sprinkle with the poppy seeds.

7 Place the parcels on a dampened baking tray and cook in a preheated oven, 200°C/400°F/Gas Mark 6, for 20 minutes, until risen and golden brown.

8 Transfer the mushroom and spinach puffs to warmed serving plates and serve immediately.

SERVES 4

25 g/1 oz butter
1 red onion, halved and sliced
2 garlic cloves, crushed
225 g/8 oz sliced open-cap mushrooms,
175 g/6 oz young spinach
pinch of ground nutmeg
4 tbsp double cream
225 g/8 oz puff pastry
1 egg, beaten
salt and pepper
2 tsp poppy seeds

NUTRITION
Calories *467*; Sugars *4 g*; Protein *8 g*;
Carbohydrate *24 g*; Fat *38 g*; Saturates *18 g*

✿✿✿   moderate
   20 mins
   30 mins

This mouthwateringly attractive tart is full of Mediterranean flavours – spinach, red peppers, ricotta cheese and pine kernels.

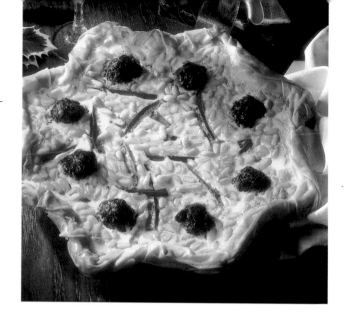

Italian Vegetable Tart

SERVES 4

225 g/8 oz frozen filo pastry, thawed
125 g/4¹/² oz butter, melted
350 g/12 oz frozen spinach, thawed
2 eggs
150 ml/5 fl oz single cream
225 g/8 oz ricotta cheese
1 red pepper, halved, deseeded and sliced into strips
55 g/2 oz pine kernels
salt and pepper

1 Use the sheets of filo pastry to line a 20-cm/8-inch flan tin, brushing each layer with melted butter.

2 Put the spinach into a strainer or colander and squeeze out the excess moisture with the back of a spoon or your hand. Form the spinach into 8–9 small balls and arrange them in the prepared flan tin.

3 Beat the eggs, cream and ricotta cheese together until thoroughly blended. Season to taste with salt and pepper and pour over the spinach.

4 Put the remaining butter into a saucepan. Add the red pepper strips and sauté them over a low heat, stirring frequently, for about 4–5 minutes, until softened. Arrange the strips on the flan.

5 Scatter the pine kernels over the surface and bake in a preheated oven, 190°C/375°F/Gas Mark 5, for about 20–25 minutes, until the filling has set and the pastry is golden brown. Serve immediately or allow to cool completely and serve at room temperature.

NUTRITION
Calories 488; Sugars 7 g; Protein 13 g; Carbohydrate 21 g; Fat 40 g; Saturates 19 g

⭐⭐⭐ moderate
🕐 30 mins
🕐 30 mins

👨‍🍳 **COOK'S TIP**

If you are not fond of peppers, you could use mushrooms instead. Wild mushrooms would be especially delicious. Add a few sliced sun-dried tomatoes for extra colour and flavour.

Different varieties of mushrooms are becoming more widely available in supermarkets, so use this recipe to make the most of them.

Mushroom Tarts

1 Cut the sheets of filo pastry into pieces about 10-cm/4-inches square and use them to line 4 individual tart tins, brushing each layer of pastry with melted butter. Line the tins with foil or baking paper and baking beans. Bake in a preheated oven, 200°C/ 400°F/Gas Mark 6, for about 6–8 minutes or until light golden brown.

2 Remove the tarts from the oven and carefully take out the foil or baking paper and baking beans. Reduce the oven temperature to 180°C/350°F/ Gas Mark 4.

3 Put any remaining butter into a large pan with the hazelnut oil and fry the pine nuts until golden brown. Remove from the pan drain on kitchen paper.

4 Add the mushrooms to the pan and cook gently, stirring frequently, for about 4–5 minutes. Add the parsley and season to taste with salt and pepper.

5 Spoon one-quarter of the goat's cheese into the base of each tart. Divide the mushrooms equally between them and sprinkle pine kernels over the top.

6 Return the tarts to the oven for about 5 minutes to heat through and then serve them, garnished with parsley sprigs. Serve with lettuce, tomatoes, cucumber and spring onions.

SERVES 4

500 g/1 lb 2 oz filo pastry, thawed if frozen
115 g/4 oz butter, melted
1 tbsp hazelnut oil
4 tbsp pine kernels
350 g/12 oz mixed mushrooms, such as button, chestnut, oyster and shiitake
2 tsp chopped fresh parsley
225 g/8 oz soft goat's cheese
salt and pepper
fresh parsley sprigs to garnish

to serve
lettuce, tomatoes, cucumber and spring onions

NUTRITION
Calories 494; Sugars 2 g; Protein 9 g; Carbohydrate 38 g; Fat 35 g; Saturates 18 g

 moderate
 15 mins
15 mins
20 mins

This is a savoury version of a cheesecake with a layer of fried potatoes as a delicious base. Use frozen mixed vegetables for the topping, if you like.

Vegetable Cake

SERVES 4

base
2 tbsp vegetable oil, plus extra for brushing
1.25 kg/2 lb 12 oz waxy potatoes, sliced thinly

topping
1 tbsp vegetable oil
1 leek, chopped
1 courgette, grated
1 red pepper, halved, deseeded and diced
1 green pepper, halved, deseeded and diced
1 carrot, grated
2 tsp chopped fresh parsley
225 g/8 oz full-fat soft cheese
4 tbsp grated mature Cheddar cheese
2 eggs, beaten
salt and pepper
shredded cooked leek, to garnish
salad, to serve

1 Brush a 20-cm/8-inch springform cake tin with oil.

2 To make the base, heat the oil in a frying pan. Cook the potato slices until softened and browned. Drain on kitchen paper and spread the potatoes in the base of the tin.

3 To make the topping, heat the oil in a separate frying pan. Add the leek and fry over a low heat, stirring frequently, for 3–4 minutes until softened.

4 Add the courgette, peppers, carrot and parsley to the pan and cook over a low heat for 5–7 minutes or until the vegetables have softened.

5 Meanwhile, beat the cheeses and eggs together in a bowl. Stir in the vegetables and season to taste with salt and pepper. Spoon the mixture evenly over the potato base.

6 Cook in a preheated oven, 190°C/375°F/Gas Mark 5, for 20–25 minutes, until the cake is set.

7 Remove the vegetable cake from the tin, transfer to a warm serving plate, garnish with shredded leek and serve with a crisp salad.

NUTRITION
Calories *502*; Sugars *8 g*; Protein *16 g*;
Carbohydrate *41 g*; Fat *31 g*; Saturates *14 g*

easy

20 mins

45 mins

Hot soufflés look very impressive if served as soon as they come out of the oven, otherwise they will sink quite quickly.

Leek *and* Herb Soufflé

1 Heat the olive oil in a frying pan. Add the leeks and sauté over a medium heat, stirring occasionally, for 2–3 minutes.

2 Add the vegetable stock to the pan, lower the heat and simmer gently for a further 5 minutes.

3 Place the walnuts in a food processor and process until chopped finely . Add the leek mixture to the nuts and process briefly to form a purée. Transfer to a mixing bowl.

4 Mix together the egg yolks, the herbs and the yogurt until thoroughly combined. Pour the egg mixture into the leek purée. Season with salt and pepper to taste and mix well.

5 In a separate, grease-free mixing bowl, whisk the egg whites until firm peaks form.

6 Fold the egg whites into the leek mixture. Spoon the mixture into a lightly greased 850 ml/1½ pint soufflé dish and place on a warmed baking tray.

7 Cook in a preheated oven, 180°C/ 350°F/Gas Mark 4, for 35–40 minutes, or until well risen and set. Serve the soufflé immediately.

S E R V E S   **4**

1 tbsp olive oil
350 g/12 oz baby leeks, finely chopped
125 ml/4 fl oz Fresh Vegetable Stock
  (see page 16)
50 g/1¼ oz walnuts
2 eggs, separated
2 tbsp chopped mixed fresh herbs
2 tbsp natural yogurt
salt and pepper

N U T R I T I O N
Calories *182*; Sugars *4 g*; Protein *8 g*;
Carbohydrate *5 g*; Fat *15 g*; Saturates *2 g*

⭐⭐⭐   moderate
    15 mins
    45-50 mins

This is a quick dish to prepare and it can be left to cook in the oven without requiring any further attention.

Cheese *and* Potato Layer Bake

SERVES 4

900 g/2 lb unpeeled waxy potatoes,
    cut into wedges
2 tbsp butter
1 red onion, halved and sliced
2 garlic cloves, crushed
2½ tbsp plain flour
600 ml/1 pint milk
400 g/14 oz canned artichoke hearts
    in brine, drained and halved
150 g/5½ oz frozen mixed
    vegetables, thawed
125 g/4½ oz Gruyère cheese, grated
125 g/4½ oz mature cheese, grated
50 g/1¾ oz Gorgonzola, crumbled
25 g/1 oz Parmesan cheese, freshly grated
225 g/8 oz tofu, sliced
2 tbsp chopped fresh thyme
salt and pepper
fresh thyme sprigs, to garnish

NUTRITION

Calories 766; Sugars 14 g; Protein 44 g;
Carbohydrate 60 g; Fat 40 g; Saturates 23 g

easy

25 mins

45 mins

1 Cook the potato wedges in a saucepan of boiling water for 10 minutes, then drain thoroughly.

2 Meanwhile, melt the butter in a saucepan. Add the sliced onion and garlic and fry over a low heat, stirring frequently, for 2–3 minutes.

3 Stir the flour into the pan and cook for 1 minute. Gradually add the milk and bring to the boil, stirring constantly.

4 Reduce the heat and then add the artichoke hearts, mixed vegetables, half of each of the 4 cheeses and the sliced tofu to the pan, mixing well to combine thoroughly.

5 Stir in the chopped thyme and season with salt and pepper to taste.

6 Arrange a layer of potato wedges in the base of a shallow ovenproof dish. Spoon the vegetable mixture over the top and cover with the remaining potato wedges. Sprinkle the rest of the 4 cheeses over the top.

7 Cook in a preheated oven, 200°C/ 400°F/Gas Mark 6, for 30 minutes, or until the potatoes are cooked and the top is golden brown. Serve the bake garnished with fresh thyme sprigs.

Fennel tastes fabulous in this creamy sauce, flavoured with caraway seeds. A crunchy breadcrumb topping gives an interesting texture.

Creamy Baked Fennel

1 Bring a saucepan of water to the boil and add the lemon juice and fennel. Cook for 2–3 minutes to blanch, drain well and place in a greased ovenproof dish.

2 Beat the soft cheese in a bowl until smooth. Add the cream, milk and beaten egg, and beat until combined. Season to taste with salt and pepper and pour the mixture over the fennel.

3 Melt 1 tablespoon of the butter in a small frying pan and fry the caraway seeds over a low heat, stirring constantly, for 1–2 minutes until they release their aroma. Sprinkle them over the fennel.

4 Melt the remaining butter in a frying pan. Add the breadcrumbs and fry over a low heat, stirring frequently, until lightly browned. Sprinkle them evenly over the top of the fennel.

5 Place in a preheated oven, 180°C/350°F/Gas Mark 4, and bake for 25–30 minutes, or until the fennel is tender. Serve immediately, garnished with parsley sprigs.

SERVES 4

2 tbsp lemon juice
2 fennel bulbs, sliced thinly
4 tbsp butter, plus extra for greasing
115 g/4 oz low-fat soft cheese
150 m/5 fl oz single cream
150 m/5 fl oz milk
1 egg, lightly beaten
2 tsp caraway seeds
55 g/2 oz fresh white breadcrumbs
salt and pepper
fresh parsley sprigs, to garnish

NUTRITION
Calories *292*; Sugars *5 g*; Protein *10 g*;
Carbohydrate *12 g*; Fat *23 g*; Saturates *14 g*

moderate
 10 mins
10 mins
35-40 mins

VEGETARIAN

Similar to a simple moussaka, this recipe is made up of layers of aubergine, tomato and potato baked with a yogurt topping.

Potato *and* Aubergine Gratin

SERVES 4

500 g/1 lb 2 oz waxy potatoes, sliced
1 tbsp vegetable oil
1 onion, chopped
2 garlic cloves, crushed
500 g/1 lb 2 oz tofu, diced
2 tbsp tomato purée
2 tbsp plain flour
300 ml/10 fl oz Fresh Vegetable Stock
   (see page 16)
2 large tomatoes, sliced
1 aubergine, sliced
2 tbsp chopped fresh thyme
450 ml/16 fl oz natural yogurt
2 eggs, beaten
salt and pepper
salad, to serve

NUTRITION

Calories 409; Sugars 17 g; Protein 28 g;
Carbohydrate 45 g; Fat 14 g; Saturates 3 g

moderate

25 mins

1 hr 15 mins

1 Cook the sliced potatoes in a saucepan of boiling water for about 10 minutes, until tender, but not breaking up. Drain and set aside.

2 Heat the oil in a frying pan. Add the onion and garlic and fry, stirring occasionally, for 2–3 minutes.

3 Add the tofu, tomato purée and flour and cook for 1 minute. Gradually stir in the stock and bring to the boil, stirring. Reduce the heat and simmer the mixture for 10 minutes.

4 Arrange a layer of the potato slices in the base of a deep ovenproof dish. Spoon the tofu mixture evenly on top. Layer the sliced tomatoes, then the aubergine and finally the remaining potato slices on top of the tofu mixture, making sure that it is completely covered. Sprinkle with thyme.

5 Mix the yogurt and beaten eggs together in a bowl and season to taste with salt and pepper. Spoon the yogurt topping over the sliced potatoes to cover them completely.

6 Bake in a preheated oven, 190°C/ 375°F/Gas Mark 5, for about 35–45 minutes or until the topping is browned. Serve with a crisp salad.

COOK'S TIP

You can use marinated or smoked tofu for extra flavour, if you wish.

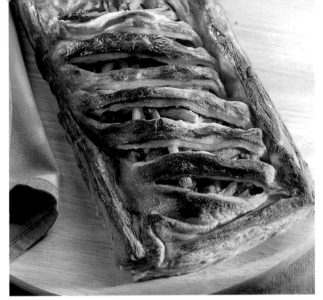

This is a really easy dish to make, but looks impressive. The mixture of vegetables gives the dish a wonderful colour and flavour.

Vegetable Jalousie

1 Melt the butter or margarine in a frying pan and sauté the leek and garlic, stirring frequently, for 2 minutes. Add the remaining vegetables and cook, stirring, for 3–4 minutes.

2 Add the flour and cook for 1 minute. Remove the pan from the heat and stir in the vegetable stock, milk and white wine. Return the pan to the heat and bring to the boil, stirring, until thickened. Stir in the oregano and season with salt and pepper to taste.

3 Roll out half of the pastry on a lightly floured surface to form a rectangle 38-cm x 15-cm/15-inches x 6-inches. Roll out the other half of the pastry to the same shape, but a little larger all round. Transfer the smaller rectangle to a baking tray lined with dampened baking parchment.

4 Spoon the filling evenly on top of the smaller rectangle, leaving a 1-cm/½-inch clear margin around the edges.

5 Using a sharp knife, cut parallel diagonal slits across the larger rectangle to within 2.5 cm/1 inch of each of the long edges.

6 Brush the edges of the smaller rectangle with beaten egg and place the larger rectangle on top, pressing the edges firmly together to seal.

7 Brush the whole jalousie with egg to glaze and bake in a preheated oven, 200°C/400°F/Gas Mark 6, for about 30–35 minutes, until risen and golden. Transfer to a warmed serving dish and serve immediately.

SERVES 4

500 g/1 lb 2 oz puff pastry
flour, for dusting
1 egg, beaten

filling
2 tbsp butter or margarine
1 leek, shredded
2 garlic cloves, crushed
1 red pepper, halved, deseeded and sliced
1 yellow pepper, halved, deseeded and sliced
50 g/1¾ oz sliced mushrooms
75 g/2¾ oz small asparagus spears
2 tbsp plain flour
6 tbsp Fresh Vegetable Stock (see page 16)
6 tbsp milk
4 tbsp dry white wine
1 tbsp chopped fresh oregano
salt and pepper

NUTRITION
Calories *660*; Sugars *7 g*; Protein *11 g*;
Carbohydrate *53 g*; Fat *45 g*; Saturates *15 g*

  moderate
  25 mins
  45 mins

This is based on a Moroccan dish in which potatoes are spiced with coriander and cumin and cooked in a lemon sauce.

Potato *and* Lemon Casserole

SERVES 4

100 ml/3½ fl oz olive oil
2 red onions, cut into 8 wedges
3 garlic cloves, crushed
2 tsp ground cumin
2 tsp ground coriander
pinch of cayenne pepper
1 carrot, sliced thickly
2 small turnips, quartered
1 courgette, sliced
500 g/1 lb 2 oz potatoes, sliced thickly
juice and rind of 2 large lemons
300 ml/10 fl oz Fresh Vegetable Stock
  (see page 16)
2 tbsp chopped fresh coriander
salt and pepper

1 Heat the olive oil in a flameproof casserole. Add the onion and sauté over a medium heat, stirring frequently, for 3 minutes.

2 Add the garlic and cook for 30 seconds. Stir in the cumin, ground coriander and cayenne and cook, stirring constantly, for 1 minute.

3 Add the carrot, turnips, courgette and potatoes and stir to coat in the oil.

4 Add the lemon juice and rind and the vegetable stock. Season to taste with salt and pepper. Cover and cook over a medium heat, stirring occasionally, for 20–30 minutes until tender.

5 Remove the lid, sprinkle in the chopped fresh coriander and stir well. Serve immediately.

NUTRITION
Calories *338*; Sugars *8 g*; Protein *5 g*;
Carbohydrate *29 g*; Fat *23 g*; Saturates *2 g*

easy
15 mins
35 mins

🍳 **COOK'S TIP**

Check the vegetables while they are cooking, because they may begin to stick to the pan. Add a little more boiling water or stock if necessary.

A mildly spiced, but richly flavoured Indian-style dish full of different textures and flavours. Serve with naan bread to soak up the tasty sauce.

Coconut Vegetable Curry

1 Layer the aubergine in a bowl, sprinkling with salt as you go. Set aside for 30 minutes. Rinse well under running water. Drain, dry on kitchen paper and set aside.

2 Heat the oil in a large saucepan and gently cook the garlic, chilli, ginger, onion and spices for 4–5 minutes.

3 Stir in the tomato purée, stock, lemon juice, potatoes and cauliflower and mix well. Bring to the boil, cover and simmer for 15 minutes.

4 Stir in the aubergine, okra, peas and coconut milk and season with salt and pepper to taste. Continue to simmer, uncovered, for a further 10 minutes until tender. Discard the cardamom pods. Pile the curry on to a warmed serving platter, garnish with flaked coconut and serve with naan bread.

SERVES 4

1 large aubergine, cut into 2.5-cm/ 1-inch cubes
2 tbsp vegetable oil
2 garlic cloves, crushed
1 fresh green chilli, deseeded and chopped finely
1 tsp grated fresh root ginger
1 onion, chopped finely
2 tsp garam masala
8 cardamom pods
1 tsp ground turmeric
1 tbsp tomato purée
700 ml/1¼ pints Fresh Vegetable Stock (see page 16)
1 tbsp lemon juice
225 g/8 oz potatoes, diced
250 g/9 oz small cauliflower florets
225 g/8 oz okra, trimmed
225 g/8 oz frozen peas
150 ml/5 fl oz coconut milk
salt and pepper
flaked coconut, to garnish
naan bread, to serve

NUTRITION
Calories 159; Sugars 8 g; Protein 8 g; Carbohydrate 19 g; Fat 6 g; Saturates 1 g

     easy

45 mins

35 mins

Quick, simple, nutritious
and a pleasure to eat –
what more could you ask
of an inexpensive midweek
meal?

Bread *and* Butter Savoury

S E R V E S 4

55 g/2 oz butter or margarine
1 bunch spring onions, sliced
6 slices of white or brown bread,
   crusts removed
175 g/6 oz grated mature Cheddar cheese
2 eggs
450 ml/16 fl oz milk
salt and pepper
flat-leaf parsley sprigs, to garnish

1 Lightly grease a 1.5 litre/2¾ pint ovenproof dish with a little of the butter.

2 Melt the remaining butter in a small saucepan. Add the spring onions and fry over a medium heat, stirring occasionally, until softened and golden.

3 Meanwhile, cut the bread into triangles and place half of them in the base of the dish. Cover with the spring onions and top with half the grated Cheddar cheese.

4 Beat together the eggs and milk and season to taste with salt and pepper. Layer the remaining triangles of bread in the dish and carefully pour over the milk mixture. Leave to soak for 15–20 minutes.

5 Sprinkle the remaining cheese over the soaked bread. Bake in a preheated oven, 190°C/375°F/Gas Mark 5, for 35–40 minutes, until puffed up and golden brown. Garnish with flat-leaf parsley and serve immediately.

N U T R I T I O N

Calories 472; Sugars 7 g; Protein 22 g;
Carbohydrate 25 g; Fat 33 g; Saturates 20 g

easy

30 mins

45 mins

🍲 **C O O K ' S   T I P**

You can vary the vegetables used in this savoury bake, depending on what you have to hand. Shallots, mushrooms or tomatoes are all suitable.

These crisp, buttery parcels, filled with nuts and pesto and served with cranberry sauce, would make a wonderful Sunday lunch.

White Nut Filo Parcels

1 Melt the butter in a frying pan, add the onion and gently fry for 2–3 minutes, until just softened, but not browned.

2 Remove from the heat and stir in the nuts, two-thirds of the breadcrumbs, the mace and beaten egg. Season to taste with salt and pepper. Set aside.

3 Place the remaining breadcrumbs in a bowl and stir in the egg yolk, pesto sauce, basil and 1 tablespoon of the melted butter. Mix well.

4 Brush 1 sheet of filo with melted butter or margarine. Fold in half and brush again. Repeat with a second sheet and lay it on top of the first one so that it forms a cross.

5 Put one-eighth of the nut mixture in the centre of the pastry. Top with one-eighth of the pesto mixture. Fold over the edges, brushing with more butter, to form a parcel. Brush the top with butter and transfer to a baking tray. Make 8 parcels in the same way and brush with the remaining butter.

6 Bake in a preheated oven, 220°C/ 425°F/Gas Mark 7, for 15–20 minutes, until golden. Transfer to serving plates, garnish with basil sprigs and serve with cranberry sauce and steamed vegetables.

SERVES 4

40 g/1½ oz butter or margarine
1 large onion, chopped finely
275 g/9½ oz mixed white nuts, such as pine kernels, unsalted cashew nuts, blanched almonds and unsalted peanuts, chopped finely
90 g/3¼ oz fresh white breadcrumbs
½ tsp ground mace
1 egg, beaten
1 egg yolk
3 tbsp pesto sauce
2 tbsp chopped basil
125 g/4½ oz butter or margarine, melted
16 sheets filo pastry
salt and pepper
fresh basil sprigs, to garnish

to serve
cranberry sauce
steamed vegetables

NUTRITION
Calories 110; Sugars 9 g; Protein 29 g; Carbohydrate 73 g; Fat 80 g; Saturates 15 g

moderate
15 mins
25 mins

This colourful combination of grated root vegetables and mixed peppers would make a stunning dinner-party dish.

Root Croustades

SERVES 4

1 orange pepper
1 red pepper
1 yellow pepper
3 tbsp olive oil
2 tbsp red wine vinegar
1 tsp French mustard
1 tsp clear honey
salt and pepper
flat-leaf parsley sprigs, to garnish
green vegetables, to serve

croustades
225 g/8 oz potatoes, coarsely grated
225 g/8 oz carrots, coarsely grated
350 g/12 oz celeriac, coarsely grated
1 garlic clove, crushed
1 tbsp lemon juice
25 g/1 oz butter or margarine, melted
1 egg, beaten
1 tbsp vegetable oil

NUTRITION
Calories *304*; Sugars *17 g*; Protein *6 g*;
Carbohydrate *28 g*; Fat *19 g*; Saturates *3 g*

moderate

2 hrs 30 mins

1 hr 15 mins

1 Place the peppers on a baking tray and bake in a preheated oven, 190°C/375°F/Gas Mark 5, for 35 minutes, turning after 20 minutes.

2 Cover with a tea towel and leave to cool for 10 minutes.

3 Peel the skin from the cooked peppers; cut in half and discard the seeds. Thinly slice the flesh into strips and place in a shallow dish.

4 Put the oil, vinegar, mustard, honey and seasoning in a small screw-top jar and shake well to mix. Pour over the pepper strips, mix well and set aside to marinate for 2 hours.

5 To make the croustades, put the grated potatoes, carrots and celeriac in a mixing bowl and toss in the crushed garlic and lemon juice.

6 Mix in the melted butter and the egg. Season to taste with salt and pepper. Divide the mixture into 8 and pile on to 2 baking trays lined with baking parchment, forming each into a 10-cm/4-inch round. Brush with oil.

7 Bake in a preheated oven, 220°C/ 425°F/Gas Mark 7, for 30–35 minutes, until the croustades are crisp around the edges and golden. Carefully transfer to a warmed serving dish.

8 Heat the peppers and the marinade for 2–3 minutes until warmed through. Spoon the peppers over the croustades, garnish with flat-leaf parsley and serve at once with green vegetables.

A delicious savoury roll, stuffed with mozzarella and broccoli. Serve as a main course or as an appetizer, in which case it would easily serve six.

Spinach Roulade

1 Wash the spinach and pack, still wet, into a large saucepan. Add the water. Cover the pan with a tight-fitting lid and cook the spinach over a high heat for 4–5 minutes, until reduced and soft. Drain thoroughly, squeezing out excess water. Chop finely and pat dry.

2 Mix the spinach with the egg yolks, seasoning and nutmeg. Whisk the egg whites until very frothy, but not too stiff, and fold into the spinach mixture.

3 Grease and line the base of a 32-cm x 23-cm/13-inch x 9-inch Swiss roll tin. Spread the mixture in the tin and smooth the surface with a wet palette knife. Bake in a preheated oven, 220°C/425°F/Gas Mark 7, for about 12–15 minutes, until firm to the touch and golden.

4 Meanwhile, cook the broccoli florets in lightly salted boiling water for 4–5 minutes, until just tender. Drain and keep the florets warm.

5 Sprinkle Parmesan on a sheet of baking parchment. Turn the base on to it and peel away the top lining paper. Sprinkle with mozzarella and top with broccoli.

6 Hold one end of the paper and roll up the spinach base like a Swiss roll. Heat the Tomato Sauce and spoon onto warmed serving plates. Slice the roulade and place on top of the tomato sauce.

SERVES 4

500 g/1 lb 2 oz small spinach leaves
2 tbsp water
4 eggs, separated
½ tsp ground nutmeg
salt and pepper
300 ml/10 fl oz Tomato Sauce (see page 16),
  to serve

filling
175 g/6 oz small broccoli florets
25 g/1 oz freshly grated Parmesan cheese
175 g/6 oz grated mozzarella cheese

NUTRITION
Calories *287*; Sugars *8 g*; Protein *23 g*;
Carbohydrate *8 g*; Fat *12 g*; Saturates *6 g*

 moderate

15 mins

25 mins

This tastes truly delicious, the flavour of roasted vegetables being entirely different from that of boiled or fried.

Roast Pepper Tart

SERVES 4

pastry
175 g/6 oz plain flour
pinch of salt
75 g/2¾ oz butter or margarine
2 tbsp green pitted olives, chopped finely
3 tbsp cold water

filling
1 red pepper
1 green pepper
1 yellow pepper
2 garlic cloves, crushed
2 tbsp olive oil
100 g/3½ oz grated mozzarella cheese
2 eggs
150 ml/5 fl oz milk
1 tbsp torn fresh basil leaves
salt and pepper

1 To make the pastry, sift the flour and salt into a bowl. Rub in the butter until the mixture resembles breadcrumbs. Add the chopped olives and cold water, bringing the mixture together to form a dough.

2 Roll the dough out on a floured surface and use to line a 20-cm/8-inch loose-based flan tin. Prick the base with a fork and leave to chill.

3 Cut the peppers in half lengthways, deseed and place them, skin side uppermost, on a baking tray. Mix the garlic and oil and brush over the peppers. Cook in a preheated oven, 200°C/400°F/ Gas Mark 6, for 20 minutes, or until beginning to char slightly.

4 Let the peppers cool slightly and thinly slice. Arrange in the base of the pastry case, layering with the grated mozzarella cheese.

5 Beat the egg and milk together and add the basil. Season and pour over the peppers. Put the tart on a baking tray and return to the oven for 20 minutes, or until set. Serve hot or cold.

NUTRITION
Calories 237; Sugars 3 g; Protein 6 g;
Carbohydrate 20 g; Fat 15 g; Saturates 4 g

moderate

25 mins

40 mins

The red of the tomatoes is a great contrast to the cauliflower and herbs, making this dish appealing to both the eye and the palate.

Cauliflower Bake

1 Cook the cauliflower in a saucepan of boiling water for 10 minutes. Drain well and reserve. Meanwhile, cook the potatoes in a pan of boiling water for 10 minutes, drain and reserve.

2 To make the sauce, melt the butter in a saucepan and sauté the leek and garlic for 1 minute. Stir in the flour and cook, stirring constantly, for 1 minute. Remove the saucepan from the heat and gradually stir in the milk, 55 g/2 oz of the cheese, the paprika and parsley. Return the saaucepan to the heat and bring to the boil, stirring constantly. Season with salt and pepper to taste.

3 Spoon the cauliflower into a deep ovenproof dish. Add the cherry tomatoes and top with the potatoes. Pour the sauce over the potatoes and sprinkle on the remaining cheese.

4 Cook in a preheated oven, 180°C/350°F/Gas Mark 4, for 20 minutes or until the vegetables are cooked through and the cheese is golden brown and bubbling. Garnish and serve immediately.

SERVES 4

500 g/1 lb 2 oz cauliflower, broken into florets
600 g/1 lb 5 oz potatoes, cubed
100 g/3½ oz cherry tomatoes

sauce

2 tbsp butter or margarine
1 leek, sliced
1 garlic clove, crushed
3 tbsp plain flour
300 ml/10 fl oz milk
85 g/3 oz mixed cheese, such as Cheddar, Parmesan and Gruyère, grated
½ tsp paprika
2 tbsp chopped fresh flat-leaf parsley
salt and pepper
chopped fresh parsley, to garnish

NUTRITION

Calories 305; Sugars 9 g; Protein 15 g; Carbohydrate 31 g; Fat 14 g; Saturates 6 g

 easy

 10 mins

10 mins

45 mins

🐢 COOK'S TIP

This dish could be made with broccoli instead of the cauliflower as an alternative.

This pastry case with a chickpea stuffing is delicious. Served with a sherry sauce and roast vegetables, it makes a tasty and impressive main dish.

Chickpea Roast

SERVES 4

450 g/1 lb canned chickpeas, drained
1 tsp yeast extract
150 g/5½ oz chopped walnuts
150 g/5½ oz fresh white breadcrumbs
1 onion, chopped finely
100 g/3½ oz mushrooms, sliced
50 g/1¾ oz canned sweetcorn, drained
2 garlic cloves, crushed
2 tbsp dry sherry
2 tbsp Fresh Vegetable Stock (see page 16)
1 tbsp chopped coriander
225 g/8 oz prepared puff pastry
1 egg, beaten
2 tbsp milk
salt and pepper

sauce
1 tbsp vegetable oil
1 leek, thinly sliced
4 tbsp dry sherry
150 ml/5 fl oz Fresh Vegetable Stock
   (see page 16)

NUTRITION

Calories *795*; Sugars *9 g*; Protein *24 g*;
Carbohydrate *66 g*; Fat *48 g*; Saturates *3 g*

⚙⚙⚙   moderate
🖐   20 mins
🕐   45 mins

1 Blend the chickpeas, yeast extract, walnuts and breadcrumbs in a food processor for 30 seconds. In a frying pan, sauté the onion and mushrooms in their own juices for 3–4 minutes. Stir in the chickpea mixture, sweetcorn and garlic. Add the sherry, stock, coriander and seasoning and bind the mixture together. Remove from the heat and allow to cool.

2 Roll the pastry out on a floured surface to form a 35.5-cm x 30-cm/ 14-inch x 12-inch rectangle. Shape the chickpea mixture into a loaf shape and wrap the pastry around it, sealing the edges. Place seam-side down on a dampened baking tray and score the top in a criss-cross pattern. Mix the egg and milk and brush over the pastry. Cook in a preheated oven, 200°C/400°F/Gas Mark 6, for 25–30 minutes.

3 To make the sauce, heat the oil in a pan and sauté the leek for 5 minutes. Add the sherry and stock, bring to the boil and simmer for 5 minutes. Place the roast on a serving platter, slice and serve with the sauce.

A tasty Mexican-style dish with a melt-in-the-mouth combination of tofu and avocado served with a delicious tomato sauce.

Chilli Tofu

1 Mix the chilli powder, paprika, flour and salt and pepper on a plate and coat the tofu pieces.

2 Heat the oil in a frying pan and gently fry the tofu for 3–4 minutes, until golden. Remove with a slotted spoon, drain on kitchen paper and set aside.

3 Add the onion, garlic and pepper to the oil and fry for 2–3 minutes, until just softened. Drain and set aside.

4 Halve the avocado, remove the stone and peel. Slice the avocado lengthways, put in a bowl with the lime juice and toss to coat.

5 Add the tofu and onion mixture and gently stir in the chopped tomatoes and half the grated Cheddar cheese. Spoon one-eighth of the filling down the centre of each tortilla, top with soured cream and roll up.

6 Arrange the tortillas in a shallow ovenproof dish in a single layer.

7 Spoon the Tomato Sauce over the tortillas, sprinkle with the remaining grated cheese and bake in a preheated oven, 190°C/375°F/Gas Mark 5, for 25 minutes, until the cheese is golden brown and bubbling.

8 Garnish the chilli tofu with coriander sprigs and serve immediately with pickled jalapeño chillies.

SERVES 4

½ tsp chilli powder
1 tsp paprika
2 tbsp plain flour
salt and pepper
225 g/8 oz tofu, cut into 1-cm/½-inch pieces
2 tbsp vegetable oil
1 onion, chopped finely
1 garlic clove, crushed
1 large red pepper, halved, deseeded and chopped finely
1 large ripe avocado
1 tbsp lime juice
4 tomatoes, peeled, deseeded and chopped
125 g/4½ oz grated Cheddar cheese
8 soft flour tortillas
150 ml/5 fl oz soured cream
850 ml/1½ pints Tomato Sauce (see page 16)
fresh coriander sprigs, to garnish
pickled green jalapeño chillies, to serve

NUTRITION
Calories 806; Sugars 20 g; Protein 37 g;
Carbohydrate 45 g; Fat 54 g; Saturates 19 g

 moderate

 30 mins

30 mins

35 mins

Salads

A salad makes a refreshing accompaniment or side dish, but can also make a substantial main course meal. Salads are also a very good source of vitamins and minerals; always use the freshest possible ingredients for maximum flavour, texture and goodness. Salads are quick to 'rustle up' and good for times when you need to prepare a meal quickly and have to use store-cupboard ingredients. A splash of culinary inspiration and you will find that you have prepared a fantastic salad that you had no idea was lurking in your kitchen! Experiment with new ingredients in order to add taste and interest to ordinary salad leaves. The only limit is your imagination!

This is a colourful salad with a Mexican theme, using beans, tomatoes and avocado. The chilli dressing adds a little kick.

Mexican Salad

SERVES 4

1 lollo rosso lettuce
2 ripe avocados
2 tsp lemon juice
4 medium tomatoes
1 onion
175 g/6 oz mixed canned beans, drained

dressing
4 tbsp olive oil
drop of chilli oil
2 tbsp garlic wine vinegar
pinch of caster sugar
pinch of chilli powder
1 tbsp chopped fresh parsley

1 Line a large serving bowl with the lettuce leaves.

2 Using a sharp knife, cut the avocados in half and remove the stones. Thinly slice the flesh and immediately sprinkle with the lemon juice.

3 Thinly slice the tomatoes and onion and push the onion out into rings. Arrange the avocado, tomatoes and onion around the salad bowl, leaving a space in the centre.

4 Spoon the beans into the centre of the salad and whisk the dressing ingredients together. Pour the dressing over the salad and serve.

NUTRITION
Calories 307; Sugars 7 g; Protein 5 g;
Carbohydrate 13 g; Fat 26 g; Saturates 5 g

 very easy

 10–15 mins

o mins

COOK'S TIP

The lemon juice is sprinkled onto the avocados to prevent discoloration when in contact with the air. For this reason the salad should be prepared, assembled and served quite quickly.

Couscous is a type of semolina made from durum wheat. It is wonderful in salads, as it readily takes up the flavour of the dressing.

Moroccan Salad

1 Put the couscous into a bowl and cover with boiling water. Leave it to soak for about 15 minutes to swell the grains, then stir gently with a fork to separate them.

2 Add the spring onions, green pepper, cucumber, chickpeas and sultanas to the couscous, stirring to combine. Season with salt and pepper.

3 To make the dressing, place the orange rind, mint and yogurt in a bowl and mix together until well combined. Pour over the couscous mixture and stir to mix well.

4 Using a sharp serrated knife, remove the peel and pith from the oranges. Cut the flesh into segments, removing all the membrane.

5 Arrange the lettuce leaves on 4 serving plates. Divide the couscous mixture between the plates and arrange the orange segments on top. Garnish with fresh mint sprigs and serve.

SERVES 4

175 g/6 oz couscous
1 bunch spring onions, finely chopped
1 small green pepper, halved, deseeded and chopped
10-cm/4-inch piece of cucumber, chopped
175 g/6 oz canned chickpeas, rinsed and drained
55 g/2 oz sultanas or raisins
2 oranges
salt and pepper
fresh mint sprigs, to garnish
lettuce leaves, to serve

dressing
finely grated rind of 1 orange
1 tbsp chopped fresh mint
150 ml/5 fl oz natural yogurt

NUTRITION
Calories *195*; Sugars *15 g*; Protein *8 g*;
Carbohydrate *40 g*; Fat *2 g*; Saturates *0.3 g*

 moderate
 30 mins
 0 mins

This attractive-looking salad can be served with a couple of vegetable kebabs for a delicious light lunch or an informal supper.

Middle Eastern Salad

SERVES 4

400 g/14 oz canned chickpeas
1 medium cucumber
4 carrots, sliced thinly
1 bunch spring onions, cut into small pieces
$^1/_2$ tsp salt
$^1/_2$ tsp pepper
3 tbsp lemon juice
1 red pepper, halved, deseeded and
   thinly sliced

1 Drain the chickpeas and place them in a large salad bowl.

2 Thickly slice the cucumber and then cut the slices into quarters. Add the carrot slices, spring onions and cucumber to the chickpeas and mix.

3 Season to taste with the salt and pepper and sprinkle with the lemon juice. Toss the salad ingredients together gently, using 2 serving spoons.

4 Arrange the slices of red pepper decoratively on top of the chickpea salad. Serve the salad immediately or chill in the refrigerator and serve when required.

NUTRITION
Calories 163; Sugars 12 g; Protein 8 g;
Carbohydrate 27 g; Fat 3 g; Saturates 0.4 g

 very easy
 15 mins
 0 mins

 **COOK'S TIP**

This salad would also be delicious made with *ful medames*. If they are not available canned, use 150 g/5$^1/_2$ oz dried, soaked for 5 hours and then simmered for 2$^1/_2$ hours.

Pecan nuts, with their slightly bitter flavour, are mixed with sweet potatoes to make a sweet and sour salad with an interesting texture.

Sweet Potato *and* Nut Salad

1 Cook the sweet potatoes in a large saucepan of boiling water for 10–15 minutes, until tender. Drain thoroughly and set aside to cool.

2 When the potatoes have cooled, stir in the celery, celeriac, spring onions and pecan nuts.

3 Line a salad plate with the chicory leaves and sprinkle with lemon juice.

4 Spoon the sweet potato mixture into the centre of the leaves.

5 In a small bowl, whisk together the vegetable oil, garlic wine vinegar, soft light brown sugar and chopped fresh thyme leaves.

6 Pour the dressing over the salad and serve at once, garnished with fresh thyme sprigs.

S E R V E S   4

500 g/1 lb 2 oz sweet potatoes, diced
2 celery sticks, sliced
125 g/4½ oz celeriac, grated
2 spring onions, sliced
50 g/1¾ oz pecan nuts, chopped
2 heads chicory, separated
1 tsp lemon juice
fresh thyme sprigs, to garnish

dressing
4 tbsp vegetable oil
1 tbsp garlic wine vinegar
1 tsp soft light brown sugar
2 tsp chopped fresh thyme

N U T R I T I O N
Calories 330; Sugars 5 g; Protein 4 g;
Carbohydrate 36 g; Fat 20 g; Saturates 2 g

  moderate

  15 mins

10–15 mins

🍳 **C O O K ' S   T I P**

Sweet potatoes do not store as well as ordinary potatoes. Store them in a cool, dark place (not the refrigerator) and use within 1 week of purchase.

This is a well-known and very popular Indonesian salad of mixed vegetables with a peanut dressing.

Gado Gado

SERVES 4

100 g/3½ oz shredded white cabbage
100 g/3½ oz French beans, cut into 3
100 g/3½ oz carrots, cut into matchsticks
100 g/3½ oz cauliflower florets
100 g/3½ oz beansprouts

dressing
100 ml/3½ fl oz vegetable oil
100 g/3½ oz unsalted peanuts
2 garlic cloves, crushed
1 small onion, chopped finely
½ tsp chilli powder
½ tsp light brown sugar
425 ml/15 fl oz water
juice of ½ lemon
salt
sliced spring onions, to garnish

1 Cook the vegetables separately in a saucepan of salted boiling water for 4–5 minutes each, drain well and chill.

2 To make the dressing, heat the oil in a frying pan and fry the peanuts, tossing frequently, for 3–4 minutes.

3 Remove from the frying pan with a slotted spoon and drain on kitchen paper. Process in a food processor or crush with a rolling pin until a fine mixture is formed.

4 Leave 1 tbsp of the oil in the pan and fry the garlic and onion for 1 minute. Add the chilli powder, light brown sugar, a pinch of salt and the water and bring to the boil.

5 Stir the peanuts into the sauce. Reduce the heat and simmer for 4–5 minutes, until the sauce thickens. Add the lemon juice and set aside to cool.

6 Arrange the vegetables in a serving dish and spoon the peanut dressing into the centre. Garnish with the sliced spring onions and serve.

NUTRITION
Calories *392*; Sugars *8 g*; Protein *9 g*;
Carbohydrate *11 g*; Fat *35 g*; Saturates *5 g*

easy

10 mins

25 mins

Fresh thin green beans are combined with soya beans and red kidney beans in a chive and tomato dressing to make a tasty salad.

Three-bean Salad

1 Put the olive oil, lemon juice, tomato purée, light malt vinegar and snipped fresh chives into a large bowl and mix thoroughly. Set aside until required.

2 Cook the thin green beans in a small pan of lightly salted boiling water for 4–5 minutes. Drain, refresh under cold water to prevent any further cooking and drain well again. Pat dry with absorbent kitchen paper.

3 Add all the beans to the dressing, stirring well to mix.

4 Add the tomatoes, spring onions and feta cheese to the bean mixture, tossing gently to coat in the dressing. Season to taste with salt and pepper.

5 Arrange the salad leaves on serving plates. Pile the bean salad on top, garnish with extra chives and serve.

SERVES 6

3 tbsp olive oil
1 tbsp lemon juice
1 tbsp tomato purée
1 tbsp light malt vinegar
1 tbsp snipped fresh chives, plus
    extra to garnish
175g/6 oz thin green beans
400 g/14 oz canned soya beans, rinsed
    and drained
400 g/14 oz canned red kidney beans,
    rinsed and drained
2 tomatoes, chopped
4 spring onions, trimmed and chopped
125 g/4½ oz feta cheese, cut into cubes
salt and pepper
mixed salad leaves, to serve

NUTRITION
Calories 276; Sugars 7 g; Protein 18 g;
Carbohydrate 18 g; Fat 15 g; Saturates 4 g

⭐⭐   easy
    10 mins
    5 mins

🍴 COOK'S TIP

For a more substantial light meal, top the salad with 2–3 sliced hard-boiled eggs and serve with crusty bread to mop up the juices.

This delicious salad combines soft goat's cheese with walnut halves, served on a bed of mixed salad leaves.

Warm Goat's Cheese Salad

SERVES 4

85 g/3 oz walnut halves
mixed salad leaves
125 g/4½ oz soft goat's cheese
snipped fresh chives, to garnish

dressing
6 tbsp walnut oil
3 tbsp white wine vinegar
1 tbsp clear honey
1 tsp Dijon mustard
pinch of ground ginger
salt and pepper

1 To make the dressing, whisk together the walnut oil, wine vinegar, honey, mustard and ginger in a small saucepan. Season to taste.

2 Heat the dressing gently, stirring occasionally, until warm. Add the walnut halves and continue to heat for 3–4 minutes.

3 Arrange the salad leaves on 4 serving plates and place spoonfuls of goat's cheese on top. Lift the walnut halves from the dressing with a draining spoon and scatter them over the salad leaves.

4 Transfer the warm dressing to a small jug. Sprinkle chives over the salads and serve with the dressing.

NUTRITION
Calories *408*; Sugars *8 g*; Protein *9 g*;
Carbohydrate *8 g*; Fat *38 g*; Saturates *8 g*

 very easy
 5 mins
5 mins

🍳 **COOK'S TIP**

You could also use a ewe's milk cheese, such as feta, in this recipe for a slightly sharper flavour.

Small new potatoes, served warm in a delicious dressing. The nutritional information is for the potato salad with the curry dressing only.

Three-way Potato Salad

1 To make the Light Curry Dressing, heat the vegetable oil in a saucepan, add the curry paste and onion and fry, stirring frequently, until the onion is soft. Remove from the heat and set aside to cool slightly.

2 Mix together the mango chutney, yogurt, cream and mayonnaise. Add the curry mixture and blend together. Season with salt and pepper.

3 To make the Vinaigrette Dressing, whisk the oil, vinegar, mustard, sugar and basil together in a small jug or bowl. Season with salt and pepper.

4 To make the Parsley Cream, combine the mayonnaise, soured cream, spring onions and parsley, mixing well. Season with salt and pepper.

5 Cook the new potatoes in lightly salted boiling water until they are just tender. Drain well and set aside to cool for 5 minutes, then add the chosen dressing, tossing to coat the potatoes thoroughly.

6 Serve the potato salad garnished with a sprinkling of chopped fresh herbs – basil or parsley, as appropriate. If you have used the Light Curry Dressing, drizzle a little single cream over the potatoes to garnish.

SERVES 4

500 g/1 lb 2 oz new potatoes for each dressing
herbs, to garnish

light curry dressing
1 tbsp vegetable oil
1 tbsp medium curry paste
1 small onion, chopped
1 tbsp mango chutney, chopped
6 tbsp natural yogurt
3 tbsp single cream
2 tbsp mayonnaise
salt and pepper
1 tbsp single cream, to garnish

vinaigrette dressing
6 tbsp hazelnut oil
3 tbsp cider vinegar
1 tsp wholegrain mustard
1 tsp caster sugar
a few basil leaves, torn

parsley cream
3 tbsp low-fat mayonnaise
150 ml/5 fl oz soured cream
4 spring onions, chopped finely
1 tbsp chopped fresh parsley

NUTRITION
Calories 310; Sugars 12 g; Protein 6 g;
Carbohydrate 31 g; Fat 19 g; Saturates 4 g

    moderate
    15 mins
          20 mins

VEGETARIAN

Use any mixture of beans you have to hand in this recipe, but the wider the variety, the more colourful the salad.

Mixed Bean *and* Apple Salad

SERVES 4

225 g/8 oz new potatoes, scrubbed and quartered
225 g/8 oz mixed canned beans, such as red kidney beans, flageolet and borlotti beans, drained and rinsed
1 red eating apple, diced and tossed in 1 tbsp lemon juice
1 yellow pepper, halved, deseeded and diced
1 shallot, sliced
½ fennel bulb, sliced
oakleaf lettuce leaves

dressing
1 tbsp red wine vinegar
2 tbsp olive oil
1½ tsp American mustard
1 garlic clove, crushed
2 tsp chopped fresh thyme

1 Cook the quartered potatoes in a saucepan of boiling water for 15 minutes until tender. Drain and transfer to a large bowl.

2 Add the mixed beans to the potatoes, with the apple, yellow pepper, shallot and fennel. Mix well, taking care not to break up the cooked potatoes.

3 To make the dressing, whisk all the dressing ingredients together until thoroughly combined, then pour it over the potato salad.

4 Line a serving plate or salad bowl with the oakleaf lettuce leaves and spoon the potato mixture into the centre. Serve the salad immediately.

NUTRITION
Calories *183*; Sugars *8 g*; Protein *6 g*; Carbohydrate *26 g*; Fat *7 g*; Saturates *1 g*

⭐ very easy
🕐 20 mins
🕐 15 mins

 COOK'S TIP

You could use Dijon or wholegrain mustard in place of American mustard.

Lightly steamed vegetables taste superb served slightly warm in a marinade of olive oil, white wine, vinegar and fresh herbs.

Marinated Vegetable Salad

1 Put the carrots, celery, sugar snap peas, fennel and asparagus into a steamer and cook over gently simmering water for 3–5 minutes until just tender. It is important that they retain a little bite.

2 Meanwhile, make the dressing. Mix together the olive oil, wine, vinegar and chopped herbs, whisking until thoroughly combined. Season to taste with salt and pepper.

3 When the vegetables are cooked, transfer them to a serving dish and immediately pour the dressing over them. The hot vegetables will absorb the flavour of the dressing as they cool.

4 Spread out the sunflower seeds on a baking sheet and toast them under a preheated grill for 3–4 minutes or until lightly browned and are beginning to smell fragrant. Sprinkle the toasted sunflower seeds over the vegetables.

5 Serve the salad while the vegetables are still slightly warm, garnished with fresh dill sprigs.

SERVES 6

175 g/6 oz baby carrots
2 celery hearts, cut into 4 pieces
115g/4 oz sugar snap peas or mangetout
1 fennel bulb, sliced
175 g/6 oz small asparagus spears
4½ tsp sunflower seeds
fresh dill sprigs, to garnish

dressing
4 tbsp extra virgin olive oil
4 tbsp dry white wine
2 tbsp white wine vinegar
1 tbsp chopped fresh dill
1 tbsp chopped fresh parsley
salt and pepper

NUTRITION
Calories 114; Sugars 4 g; Protein 3 g;
Carbohydrate 5 g; Fat 9 g; Saturates 1 g

 easy

 10 mins

10 mins

This refreshing salad must be assembled just before serving to prevent all of the ingredients being coloured pink by the beetroot.

Alfalfa *and* Beetroot Salad

SERVES 4

100 g/3½ oz young spinach leaves
85 g/3 oz alfalfa sprouts
2 celery sticks, sliced
4 cooked beetroot, cut into 8 wedges

dressing
4 tbsp olive oil
4½ tsp garlic wine vinegar
1 garlic clove, crushed
2 tsp clear honey
1 tbsp chopped fresh chives

1 If the spinach leaves are large, tear them into smaller pieces. (Cutting them would bruise them.) Place the spinach and alfalfa sprouts in a large bowl and mix together.

2 Add the celery and mix well. Toss in the beetroot and mix again.

3 To make the dressing, mix the oil, wine vinegar, garlic, honey and chopped chives in a small bowl.

4 Pour the dressing over the salad, toss well and serve immediately.

NUTRITION
Calories *139*; Sugars *7 g*; Protein *2 g*;
Carbohydrate *8 g*; Fat *11 g*; Saturates *2 g*

very easy

10 mins

0 mins

COOK'S TIP

Add the segments of 1 large orange to the salad to make it even more colourful and refreshing. Replace the garlic wine vinegar with plain white wine vinegar and use a different flavoured oil such as chilli or herb, if you prefer.

This salad uses lots of green-coloured ingredients which look and taste wonderful with the minty yogurt dressing.

Courgette *and* Mint Salad

1 Cook the courgette batons and beans in a saucepan of lightly salted boiling water for 7–8 minutes. Drain, rinse under cold running water and drain again. Set aside to cool completely.

2 Mix the courgettes and beans with the green pepper strips, celery and watercress in a large serving bowl.

3 To make the dressing, combine the natural yogurt, garlic and chopped mint in a small bowl. Season the dressing with pepper to taste.

4 Spoon the dressing onto the salad and serve immediately.

SERVES 4

2 courgettes, cut into batons
100 g/3½ oz French beans, cut into thirds
1 green pepper, halved, deseeded and cut into strips
2 celery sticks, sliced
1 bunch of watercress

dressing
200 ml/7 fl oz natural yogurt
1 garlic clove, crushed
2 tbsp chopped fresh mint
pepper

NUTRITION
Calories 49; Sugars 5 g; Protein 4 g; Carbohydrate 6 g; Fat 1 g; Saturates 0 g

 very easy

 30 mins

7–8 mins

🍴 COOK'S TIP

The salad must be served as soon as the yogurt dressing has been added – the dressing will start to separate if it is kept for any length of time.

This refreshing fruit-based salad is perfect for a hot summer's day.

Melon *and* Strawberry Salad

S E R V E S   4

½ iceberg lettuce, shredded
1 small honeydew melon
225 g/8 oz strawberries, sliced
5-cm/2-inch piece of cucumber, sliced thinly
fresh mint sprigs, to garnish

dressing
200 g/7 fl oz natural yogurt
5-cm/2-inch piece of cucumber, peeled
a few fresh mint leaves
½ tsp finely grated lime or lemon rind
pinch of caster sugar
3–4 ice cubes

1 Arrange the shredded lettuce on 4 serving plates.

2 Cut the melon lengthways into quarters. Scoop out the seeds and cut through the flesh down to the skin at 2.5-cm/1-inch intervals. Cut the melon close to the skin and detach the flesh.

3 Place the chunks of melon on the beds of lettuce with the strawberries and cucumber slices.

4 To make the dressing, put the yogurt, cucumber, mint leaves, lime rind, caster sugar and ice cubes into a blender or food processor. Blend together for about 15 seconds until smooth. Alternatively, chop the cucumber and mint finely, crush the ice cubes and combine those with the other ingredients.

5 Serve the salad with a little dressing poured over it. Garnish with fresh mint sprigs.

N U T R I T I O N
Calories *112*; Sugars *22 g*; Protein *5 g*; Carbohydrate *22 g*; Fat *1 g*; Saturates *0.3 g*

very easy

15 mins

0 mins

🍲 **C O O K ' S   T I P**

Omit the ice cubes from the dressing if you prefer, but make sure that the ingredients are well-chilled, to ensure that the finished dressing is really cool.

A little freshly grated root ginger mixed with creamy yogurt and clear honey makes a perfect dressing for this refreshing salad.

Melon *and* Mango Salad

1 To make the dressing, for the melon, whisk together the yogurt, honey and ginger in a small bowl.

2 Halve the melon, scoop out the seeds with a spoon and discard. Slice, peel and dice the flesh. Place in a bowl with the grapes.

3 Slice the mango on each side of its large flat stone. On each mango half, slash the flesh into a criss-cross pattern down to, but not through the skin. Push the skin from underneath to turn the mango halves inside out. Now remove the flesh and add to the melon mixture.

4 Arrange the watercress and lettuce leaves on 4 serving plates.

5 Whisk together the olive oil and vinegar with a little salt and pepper. Drizzle over the salad leaves.

6 Divide the melon mixture between the 4 plates and spoon over the yogurt dressing.

7 Scoop the seeds out of the passion fruit and sprinkle them over the salads. Serve immediately or chill in the refrigerator until required.

SERVES 4

1 cantaloupe melon
55 g/2 oz black grapes, halved and deseeded
55 g/2 oz green grapes
1 large mango
1 bunch of watercress, trimmed
iceberg lettuce leaves, shredded
2 tbsp olive oil
1 tbsp cider vinegar
1 passion fruit
salt and pepper

dressing
150 ml/5 fl oz low-fat natural yogurt
1 tbsp clear honey
1 tsp grated fresh root ginger

NUTRITION
Calories *189*; Sugars *30 g*; Protein *5 g*;
Carbohydrate *30 g*; Fat *7 g*; Saturates *1 g*

⊗⊗   easy
       15 mins
     20 mins

Index